The Guardian Angel

Every Entrepreneur Needs One

By

H. Randall Goldsmith, PhD

H. Randall Goldsmith, PhD
C/O Mississippi Technology Alliance
134 Market Ridge Drive
Ridgeland, Mississippi 39157

www.mta.ms

ISBN 978-0-615-31273-6

Chapter 1

The Adventure Begins

Max Grant pulled into the parking garage just as he had done several thousand times before. As he took the elevator ride to the 27th floor, he thought about his construction projects scattered around the world, as he had done daily for the last forty years. When he walked into the office, he greeted Roberta, his administrative assistant, as he had done every day before. Max had no reason to believe this day would be the first day of a new adventure. It began with a phone call.

"Good morning, Mr. Grant, your nephew, Jack, is holding on line one."

"Jumpin' Jack!" answered Max, with pleasure at knowing his favorite nephew was on the other end of the line.

"Uncle Max!" responded Jack, with matching enthusiasm.

Had outsiders been listening, they would have intuitively perceived the genuine affection between the two.

"To what do I owe the pleasure?"

"I'd like to find a time to get on your calendar, Uncle Max."

"Sure, anytime, but why don't you just drop by the house?"

"I don't have time to explain why right now, but I'd really rather meet during business hours if that's ok with you."

"No problem for me. Make it easy on yourself." Jack's business-like manner made Max think about how Jack had grown into a young professional who carried himself exceptionally well. People liked Jack. Max silently muttered to himself, *Jack is the real deal*, a favorite phrase he invariably uttered when thinking about the boy since he was a toddler.

Jack had graduated from college with a degree in computer science. Now the father of two little boys with a darling wife, he had a solid job with a strong company, his father's heavy equipment manufacturing business. His rise through the ranks to vice president of operations was not gratuitous. Jack had made significant innovative changes to the 60-year-old company from the summer between his sophomore and junior years in high school, when he had accepted a part-time entry-level position as a stock boy.

John Grant Sr., Max's father, had started Grant International Equipment just after World War II ended. Taking advantage of a booming post-war economy, John Sr. was able to grow the company into an international powerhouse. Max had grown up in the business with his older brother, John Jr. The boys had started at the bottom of the ladder and had worked up to middle management roles before either finished undergraduate studies. In college, John Jr. took the business route, graduating with a master's in business administration degree, while Max took the engineering route with a degree in construction engineering. Their father passed away unexpectedly after both boys had reached senior management levels in the company. Max was the first to propose that John Jr. buy out his interest in the company.

By recognizing that both brothers were highly competitive, extremely bright, and ambitious, Max knew neither brother would be satisfied with anything less than being *the* boss. It turned out to be a good decision all the way around. John Jr. continued to grow the manufacturing business, and Max had built an extraordinarily successful road construction company.

Thinking about John Sr. and John Jr. reminded Max of the day when John Grant III made a declaration at the age of seven. From that day forth, he would be known as Jack. It was the same day Max tagged him with the nickname Jumpin' Jack. Somehow, Max knew this young man with a mind of his own and unbridled energy would be different, if not exceptional.

Jack was an all-American kid. He never demonstrated any serious signs of rebellion, unruliness, or misbehavior. He participated in organized sports, extracurricular school programs, and loved reading. Blessed with superior social skills and considered a leader among his peers, Jack's most defining personal characteristic was competitiveness. It did not matter whether it was a game of checkers at the age of eight, shooting hoops at fifteen, or growing his career at the age of twenty-three. Every situation had the potential for competition, if Jack could find an opponent.

"Thanks, Uncle Max! Gotta run. I look forward to seeing you soon."

"Sounds great, Jack. I'll send you back to Roberta and you guys find us a time to meet."

The following week, Roberta announced Jack's arrival.

"Jumpin' Jack!"

"Uncle Max!"

As the two men gave each other bear hugs, Roberta giggled to herself. She enjoyed seeing Max Grant show his affectionate side. It was not an everyday occurrence for this business and civic tycoon. His personality was a contradiction in concepts. On one hand, he was a tough businessperson, a frugal investor, and a critical thinker. At the same time, he was considered a modest man. Quick to give others credit, lend his name and money to causes he believed in, and keep his priorities in proper order, all knew him as polite, generous, respectful and passionate. Yet no one would describe him as outwardly affectionate.

Max led Jack to a matching leather couch and club chair arrangement in the corner of his spacious office. As Jack sank into the soft material, he absorbed the vast amount of memorabilia that adorned the walls, bookcases, side tables and his uncle's massive desk. Dozens of photos of celebrities, politicians, and customers memorialized his multifaceted and successful career. It was a walk down Memory Lane and a Who's Who gallery at the same time. Toy-size bulldozers, dump trucks, motor graders, front-end loaders and a plethora of other miniature replicas of heavy equipment brands filled the room. A grateful sales person had presented each one to Max with some fanfare whenever Max made one of his numerous purchases. Seeing the souvenirs reminded Jack how much his boys enjoyed visiting Max's office when they were toddlers. It was a virtual playground for tiny tykes.

The surroundings triggered Max's memories as well. "How are the boys, Jack?"

"Just great, Uncle Max." Jack's eyes lit up, just talking about them. "Between soccer, scouts, karate, and school stuff, Liz and I have no time to catch a breath, and they're growing like weeds. We don't even take the tags off Gray's new school clothes. That way, Noah thinks the hand-me-downs are new."

Max laughed, not because it was a funny thought, but because of the knowledge that Jack would be more in favor of the concept if it weren't for Liz putting her foot down. "Tell 'em I intend to have them up to the lake this summer to ski."

"They'd love it, Uncle Max!" Jack grinned. Max's place on the lake was like a luxury resort, and Jack and the family always had a memorable time there.

After a slight pause, Jack turned serious. "Uncle Max, let me cut to the chase. I'd like to borrow some money."

Max's head bobbled and his eyes blinked as if a raindrop had splattered between his eyes. "Say what?" The exclamation spilled out before Max's mind could pre-approve the words.

"Yes, Uncle Max, I said borrow some money," Jack said, with a tight, narrow smile.

As Max asked the purpose, his mind was already racing. Knowing that Jack had a great job, good income, and a father with as much wealth as himself, Max anticipated hearing an unpleasant answer.

Jack took a deep breath. "I want to borrow money to start a business, Uncle Max."

Once again and as if spoken by someone else in the room, Max's words "Say what?" were louder and an octave higher.

"Yes, a business," Jack said, with a childish look of cautious anticipation on his face.

Max took a deep breath and purposely exhaled slowly and deliberately. "Jack, you could knock me over with a feather right now. What makes you think you want to start a business?"

"It's an urge to do something my own. I need to feel like I've made something of myself on my own," Jack said, as his countenance shifted to one of serious consideration while anticipating his uncle's response.

Max carefully considered his words. "Jack, your motivation may or may not be a good reason, but let's come back to that later. I know you know that you have an enviable business future in front of you. Your dad's company will be yours one day. He's counting on you to be the third John Grant to lead the family business."

"I know, Uncle Max," Jack replied, as he slipped a vibrating Blackberry off his belt to see who was calling. Noting that he could return the call later, he continued. "But I need to create something on my own, to be my own man. With Dad's good health and joy for work, it could be another 20 years before he decides to retire."

Max paused to contemplate his response. He softly pinched his lower lip between his thumb and forefinger, a habit he had developed over the years when drilling into rational analysis. In soft, measured tones, Max said, "Jack, what you are saying is that you want to be an entrepreneur."

Jack cocked his head to the right, glanced upward and to the left, and furrowed his brow while investigating the comment. After a moment, he said, "I never thought about the entrepreneur label, but, yes, I guess so, just like you and Dad."

"Well, yes and no," Max replied. "You see, there's a subtle distinction that you need to understand between me and your dad. Obviously, he is a very good businessman in every sense of the word. He's not an entrepreneur, though, at least not by my definition." Max paused for a moment to search again for the right words. "An entrepreneur is a person who assumes the risk for creating and managing a business. The key differentiating word is *creating*. Creating the business connotes a risk level that far exceeds the risk associated with managing the business. Your dad assumed the business after it was well established and far beyond the question of whether it would succeed or fail. He's done a wonderful job of building on the foundation established by our father, who was the entrepreneur. You know, I heard someone say once that 'pessimists are people who find problems in every opportunity, and entrepreneurs are people who find opportunity in every problem.' That saying always comes to my mind when I think about my dad and his business."

Jack sat for a moment considering what he had heard. "Entrepreneur," Jack said softly to himself, as if rolling the term around in his head to see it in three dimensions, to try it on for size, and to feel its weight and texture. "Yes, definitely. I want to be an entrepreneur."

"Jack, many a man have sat where you're sitting and asked me for money. Some of those men are fabulously successful today, and you would know them by name and reputation. Some good men you'll never know because they weren't successful. Success is not entirely dependent on talent, skill, and determination." Sometimes, Max had learned, forces much greater than the entrepreneur intervene to derail the best-laid plans.

"I know you're anxiously awaiting me to ask you about your business idea, and I'm anxious to know. However, I'm going to disappoint you. I'm not going to ask just yet. Instead, I'm going to assign you some homework. First, I want you to do some research on three of my favorite entrepreneurs: Eli Whitney, inventor of the cotton gin; Milton Hershey, the founder of the chocolate candy industry; and Chester Carlson, inventor of the photocopier. As you read about them, get inside their heads, feel their frustration, their trials and tribulations, sense their fear and anxiety as well as their elation. Second, I want you to interview two or three entrepreneurs. One who is pre-profitable and still in the early stages of the company, and one who is now profitable. Let them tell you their stories. Third, I want you to take a little survey that assesses your credentials, circumstances, character, capabilities, and commitment to be an entrepreneur. It will give you a score somewhere between one and 100, based on your inclinations. Fourth, I want you think about the effects it will have on your life if you aren't successful and how you would recover. Fifth, after you've done these four things, I want you to have a very serious discussion with Liz, and tell her all of the things that could go wrong, and see if she is okay with you being a mentally absentee husband and father for the next year, because you'll be present in body, but absent in spirit. Finally, the sixth thing. If after you've done all of these assignments and you still want to go forward, call me and we'll meet again."

Chapter 2
The Entrepreneur

"Order up!" came a shout through a wall opening separating the diner from the kitchen.

Jack smiled to himself as he thought about how symbolic this old cafe was of his Uncle Max. It had to be older than Max. It looked like a place you would see in a 1950s-era movie. Fake leather covered backless stools that could spin like a top lined the dining counter. A place setting of salt, pepper, sugar, ketchup, hot sauce, and a menu was perfectly ordered between seats. Along the outside wall, six booths with laminate plastic tables rimmed with stainless steel trim provided additional seating. Jack was fascinated with the countertop jukebox attached to each table. As he made himself comfortable in his uncle's favorite booth, Jack flipped through the folio of music pages safely ensconced inside the colorful antique, recognizing some old tunes. He wanted to put a quarter in the device and make a selection just for the fun of it, but quickly decided it wasn't the right time.

"Jack, I've been eating breakfast here at least once a week for my entire life. I used to come here when I was a teenager to get pork chops and gravy during the summer when dad had me on the early shift. It has not changed one iota in all these years. This place keeps me connected to many wonderful old memories." Max smiled and looked Jack directly in the eyes. "You're the first person I've invited into my sanctuary."

Then Max shifted his tone to one of strictly business. "Well, you've had two weeks to work through your assignment. Tell me what you've learned."

"It was a great assignment, Uncle Max. The survey looked simple at first and I found myself providing responses that would make me look good in your eyes. However, the farther I got into it, the more I realized the intent of the questions were to stimulate a deeper reflection into my motivation to be an entrepreneur. It became clear that the intent of the effort was to help me be comfortable with my decision and not you. So I started over."

"Well, what was the outcome?"

"I was disappointed that I didn't score high enough to be 'investor ready.' I scored 82, which said I met the criteria to be a high performance entrepreneur, whatever that means."

Max smiled. "Eighty-two is good. A high performance entrepreneur simply means you demonstrate the personal criteria to launch and manage a company with fast growth potential. You'll be interested to know that I scored a 78."

A big grin erupted on Jack's face. "Cool!" he said, with some sense of relief.

"There was a time I would've scored higher and other times when I might've scored lower. It's a relative assessment, depending on what's going on in your life, your stage of life, pressing priorities, and a bunch of other stuff. Since the answers to the questions are all designed to reflect an investor's highest expectation, the final result is designed to give us insight into how an investor would perceive your ability to lead one of their companies."

Mildred, Max's favorite waitress, arrived at the table wearing a stiffly starched coral uniform with a crisp white apron tied around her waist "Max, you want your usual?"

"Yep, two over easy with bacon and…."

"Rye toast," Mildred and Max said in unison.

She turned to Jack. "What about you?"

"I'll have the fruit cup and oatmeal."

"Geez," muttered Max, shaking his head. *Why are kids these days so afraid to eat a hearty breakfast?*

"What did you learn from the reading assignment?" Max asked, as he slid a napkin under his cup to absorb Mildred's miscalculation of a few drops of coffee.

"Very interesting reading. I learned from Whitney's experience that fame and reputation do not necessarily translate into financial reward. From Hershey, I learned a couple of things. Good guys can win and if something knocks you down, you can still get up and succeed. From Carlson, I learned success can take a long time and the opportunity costs can be very high."

"Well done. I could not have summarized it better myself," Max said, thoughtfully. "Okay then. What about your interviews?"

"That was a fascinating exercise. I have a good friend from college who has built a very successful restaurant chain. He started with one operation twelve years ago and now has seven locations. I went by his corporate headquarters and got a great briefing on his operations. When I asked what he liked best about the business, he said 'it stimulates my creativity.' When I asked what that meant, he said the restaurant business is dependent on the customer experience. It requires keeping the facilities, the menu, the presentation, the ambiance, and the advertising fresh and new. He said that we have to greet our customers with something different every quarter of the year to stay ahead of the competition."

"He's right. The restaurant business probably has the highest mortality rate on the planet. I can only pray you aren't thinking about opening a restaurant!"

"Oh no," Jack said, with a tone of reassurance. "When I asked what he liked least, he asked me jokingly how much time I had to talk. He said his greatest disappointment was not having the opportunity to manage a restaurant, the very thing that got him in the business to begin with. He said he is now in the business of business. On a more serious note, he didn't like the pressure of being responsible for the livelihood of so many employees and the fact that the business is always on his mind 24/7."

"That's generally a unanimous response among entrepreneurs."

Jack continued. "When I asked if it was worth it, he said emphatically yes! He loved it. It defined him. He was making great money. It gave him credibility in the community. But most of all, and he struggled some with his explanation, he said it gave him a great sense of value to see happy customers."

"Good. What about the startup interview?"

"That took a little effort. I had to find one, but after a few inquiries, I networked into an organization that works with startups, one that helps with business plans, funding and other stuff. It'll be a good resource for me. Anyway, they had a bunch to choose from and were pleased to facilitate an introduction when I told them about my quest."

Jack spent the next ten minutes explaining what he had learned from his meeting with a startup software company and their challenges. He related with empathy the daunting challenges that faced the entrepreneur in developing a business plan, securing funding, developing a marketing strategy, bringing their product to market, putting the business systems in place, finding vendors, and incurring a whole host of other challenges.

After finishing his report, Max asked, "Well, what thoughts did you walk away with?"

Jack answered with a smile while shaking his head, indicating near disbelief. "Uncle Max, you'd think this guy had died and gone to heaven. He's as happy as a pig in the sunshine!"

Max laughed aloud.

"When I came home and told Liz about my discussion, she said I was glowing with enthusiasm. Of course, that was a perfect lead in to my discussion with Liz. We had a long talk about our future. Once we got into the discussion, it became clear that this is not a trivial decision. We could lose money. It could threaten our relationship. It will, one way or another, for better or worse, affect our lives."

"Well, what was your final decision?"

"We decided we must be practical about this. We agreed that we'd give it a year. If after twelve months we aren't in mutual agreement," Jack paused for emphasis, "we'll pull the plug. She's excited about my idea and has a lot of trust in me. But I'll tell you, Uncle Max, this was a sobering process. It caused me to really think through the implications."

"Jack, I find your consistent use of the word 'we' comforting. One way or another, Liz is going to be your partner in this adventure. Never forget for a moment, her sacrifices will be just as great as yours."

After taking a sip of steaming coffee, Max said: "Okay, the time has come. Tell me about your idea."

Jack took a deep breath, ratcheting up his courage. "Uncle Max," Jack started slowly and deliberately, "I want to start a car company."

"Say what?" Startled by the statement, Max's body suddenly shifted forward, rattling spoons, forks, cups and plates on the table as he bumped it involuntarily. He moved closer to Jack. "Are you nuts?"

Jack instinctively retreated, but quickly regained his composure. "Uncle Max, you're gonna love what I'm going to tell you."

"Okay. Let's hear it."

Jack's monologue on his new car idea, interrupted with a couple of twitters and a cell call, rambled for more than twenty minutes. As Jack described the features, benefits, market, business model, designs, vendors, workforce and assembly concept mixed with quotes from Henry Ford and Lee Iacocca, Max found himself nodding in agreement with much of Jack's idea. Jack, not giving Max a moment to get in a word edgewise, regurgitated nearly every concept, thought, belief, feeling, fact and figure he had collected for the last six months.

Max finally raised his hand in traffic cop fashion, signaling Jack to stop. "Well, Jack, there might be a pony in there somewhere."

Jack wondered about Max's statement. He was notorious for dropping phrases that must have meaning only to Max.

"You've obviously given this a tremendous amount of research and thought. As shocked as I was initially, I must confess the idea intrigues me. Your deal reminds me of a favorite quote of mine: 'Make no small plans, for they have not the power to stir men's imagination.' It certainly applies in your circumstance. However, let me be candid with you. Most investors will tell you it's suicide to attempt to penetrate a mature market dominated by large corporations. You might get a few scraps, but never large market share unless you're radically different. Second, you have no automotive experience, but your heavy equipment manufacturing background will get you points. Third, you'd better have a defendable competitive advantage that no one can take away from you. Fourth, it's a low margin, high volume business. Fifth, I expect the startup costs to be horrendous! I could probably come up with ten more reasons, but five is a good beginning."

Max had always held to the theory that great opportunities present themselves when great companies get complacent and satisfied. When companies stop innovating, they become vulnerable to sliding down the slippery slope toward obsolescence. Jack's idea was truly a David and Goliath concept, but given the global uncertainty and systemic disruption in the automotive industry, a small company might stand a chance.

"Jack, you initially indicated that you wanted to borrow some money for this idea. Tell me what you're thinking about."

Jack danced around the question, not to evade an answer but out of uncertainty. Numbers for various aspects of the business ranged from several hundred thousand to several million dollars.

When Jack did not answer immediately, Max said: "Jack, what I hear you saying is you aren't sure. However, let me say this. I'm not interested in loaning you a hundred thousand dollars, much less a million or more."

As Jack began to show a depressing feeling of defeat, Max rescued him with a single word, "But...." Max paused to critically assess his commitment to what he was about to say. "That doesn't mean I'm turning you down. The reason I'm not interested in loaning you the money is this. Business is business, and family is family. If I loan you a lot of money, it means you have to pay me back at a risk-adjusted interest rate. Do you know how much money you'd have to earn and how long it would take you to repay one hundred thousand dollars plus interest? I can tell you the answer: a lot and forever. In addition, imagine having the obligation if you were unsuccessful, if your venture was a complete flop. I promise you, in your heart, you'd be hoping I'd take sympathy on you and forgive the debt. When I didn't, our feelings toward each other would change. I'd be better off giving you the money as a gift. I know that's not what I want, and I don't think it's what you want. I like you but not enough to give you a hundred thou, sonny!"

Both men laughed.

Mildred filled both cups of coffee and laid a ticket on the table with $6.75 scribbled on it.

"Let me get that, Uncle Max," Jack said, reaching for the check.

"Not this time, Jack, but next time for sure. Here's what we're gonna do. I think your idea has merit and maybe for reasons you aren't aware of. As I said, I'm not interested in loaning you money."

Max paused to be sure Jack was anticipating his words. "But I might be interested enough to invest in your deal."

"What's the difference?"

"A lot. If you're willing, I'm willing to work with you to see if this pony will run."

Geez, thought Jack, *another pony deal!*

"Your next assignment is to determine whether you want to pursue this effort with debt or equity financing. Before we meet again, I want you to investigate some new subjects: angel investors, private equity financing, venture valuation, venture capital, venture capitalists, IPOs, mergers, and acquisitions. Second, I want you to talk with an angel investor. I don't want you to pitch your deal to him. I want you to discover what criteria he uses to make an investment decision. What kinds of deals he looks for. How much money he usually invests. Learn everything you can learn. I'll leave it to you to discover how to find one."

Jack took notes on the back of a napkin.

"We'll meet next week. Same time. Same place."

Chapter 3
The Investor

"Mildred, forget the fruit cup and the oatmeal. Bring this young man your ironworker's breakfast."

"No, no, please," pleaded Jack. "The fruit cup will be fine."

"Jack, indulge me just this one time. I want you to experience something special. I'll never insist again."

"What is it?"

"You'll see."

"Okay Mildred, make mine the ironworker," Jack said, with a forced smile.

Quickly shifting gears, Max asked, "Well, you've had a week to learn all there is to learn about equity investment. How did it go?"

"It went really well. I learned a ton. It really opened my eyes. Even though I'm familiar with stocks and mutual funds, I'm surprised at how ignorant I was on the subject."

"It's important for me to know you have a thorough understanding of private investment. I have a couple of key questions for you today. The first is: do you want to finance your car company with debt or equity?"

"I'm definitely interested in equity financing, Uncle Max."

Jack spent several minutes offering a convincing explanation of his logic on why equity financing was the best option for his venture. It was clear to Max that Jack was a quick study and picked up easily on the concept of equity financing and the investment process. Jack did not stop talking until Mildred slid the ironworker breakfast in front of him. Jack looked down and tried to conceal a look of disgust. A pair of fried eggs on two small pork chops resting on a bed of cheese grits stared back at him. In addition to the entree was a separate plate with two biscuits and a bowl of cream gravy. How many calories and fat grams were on these two plates? Jack wondered how many hours in the gym would be required to reverse what he was about to do.

"While you eat, I'll do most of the talking but first, I have another question for you," said Max.

"Ask away. I'll try to answer in between pork chops."

"What are investors primarily interested in?"

As Max posed his question, Jack's cell phone began to vibrate on the tabletop. "Hold on a sec, Uncle Max." Max overheard Jack chatting with someone about a tee time for Saturday morning.

"Sorry about that. What was the question again?"

"What are investors primarily interested in?"

"Money!" Jack said, with a twinkle in his eye. "They expect a high return on their money. All of my reading and research suggests it's almost an obsession. I mean, expecting a return on investment ten times their original investment seems excessive."

"Well, let me help you with some perspective. Listen closely because your understanding and comfort level with investment concepts will greatly affect your ability for funding. I'll personalize it for you. I worked hard to make money. Now, my money makes money for me. That's no accident. It was a strategy drilled into me by your grandfather when I was young, and one I expect you to pass on to your boys."

"Yep, dad tells me often how you and he set up your savings accounts at the age of nine," Jack interjected.

"Now I have money to manage, and here's the way I do it. I want my money to grow, but at my age, I've become increasingly more conservative because you never know what the future holds. I put ninety-five percent of my wealth in a diversified portfolio of ultra-safe, safe, and moderately risky investments. My ultra-safe investments are in certificates of deposit, municipal bonds, and treasuries. I expect to average a return of about five to seven percent per year."

Max continued. "Another category is real estate like my home, lake house, office building, commercial warehouses, and some raw land. Some of these you would consider safe and others moderately risky. One of the good things about real estate is that you can touch it and feel it. It's real property. At a minimum, I expect my real estate to appreciate at a rate equal to inflation. On the other hand, I buy raw land to double or triple my money over a five-year holding period. So when I analyze my real estate holdings,

I'm looking for an average annual return of around ten percent per year."

Jack interrupted. "What percentage of a portfolio do you recommend for real estate investments, Uncle Max?"

"I'll get to that in a minute. Another category is stocks and mutual funds. Again, these range from blue chips to riskier ones like emerging markets. Some are riskier than others, but I have an overall expectation to equal or beat the market average each year by a couple of percentage points. I'm generally looking for an annual return of fifteen percent. So you can see my expected return on all my investments averages about ten to twelve percent per year. Now, here's a trivia question for you. If I average a twelve percent return per year, how many years will it take for me to double my money excluding any tax implications?"

The question caught Jack by surprise. "Umm, I don't know, maybe ten?" If he had brought his calculator, Jack was sure he could have answered the question in no time.

"Six!" Max paused for effect. "It's based on the law of seventy-two. Don't ask me how it works, but don't forget it. If you want to figure out how quickly your money will double, divide the interest rate into the number seventy-two. Twelve percent into seventy-two equals six. Likewise, if you want to know what interest rate you need to earn to double your money within a specific period, divide the number of years into seventy-two. Six years divided into seventy-two equals twelve percent."

"That's easy enough, but what about the other five percent of your investment portfolio?"

"Patience," Max chided Jack playfully. "And don't forget my lesson on seventy-two. I invest the remaining five percent in what investors call alternative asset class investments, collectibles and other miscellaneous investments. I have a nice collection of art, wines, and jewelry, but most of it is in venture investments. There are multiple classifications of ventures, and all have a risk aspect to them. For instance, one classification is by sector like software, retail, construction, medical devices or energy. Some sectors are riskier than others in creating the venture and bringing a product to market."

"Yeah, I picked up on that," Jack noted. "Biotech companies are a lot riskier than software."

"Precisely, Jack. It's not rocket science, is it? So if you had a choice to invest in a software startup or a biotech startup, it's obvious with all things being equal that the biotech startup has the higher risk profile. Right?"

"Right," Jack concurred. "Biotech has FDA requirements and clinical trials, lots of money, lots of risk."

"So if you invested in the biotech company instead of the software company, you would expect a higher rate of return to offset the risk, right?"

"Right again. But how do you calculate the risk difference?"

"Patience, Jack. In addition to sector risk, you have stage risk. Stage risk refers to whether the company is a startup, one that is already profitable, or somewhere in between. Startups are obviously riskier than profitable companies. Then there's venture risk. Every venture has a unique risk profile related to five risk factors—product or service, market, management, finance, and execution. So you can see that calculating a risk factor is complicated and more of an art than a science."

"Geez, Uncle Max, so what do you do. Guess at it?" asked Jack, as he cut into his second pork chop.

"Oh no. There are some tried and true methods to determine risk, but we'll get into that at the right time. The point I want you to understand is that every venture has a different risk profile, and investors have different levels of risk tolerance. My assessment of the risk level will determine whether my expected compounded rate of return is twenty-five percent or fifty percent."

"I completely understand," Jack assured his uncle.

"Now, there's one more thing to add. If your total net worth were one million dollars, you wouldn't invest it all in a single, high-risk investment like a stock or a piece of real estate. Likewise, investors don't invest in one venture. In fact, we have a rule of thumb called the 2-6-2 rule, meaning two investments will fail, six will be okay but not spectacular, and two will do well and make up for the others."

"That doesn't seem like a good ratio," Jack observed.

"Well, bear with me and I'll show you some quick math."

"Are you gonna use the rule of seventy-two on me?" Jack asked, chuckling.

"No," Max replied, laughing. Then he turned serious again. "Let's say an investor has five investments. One will probably be a winner. Let's say the investor invests a hundred thousand dollars in each deal, with an expectation of getting a twenty-five percent compounded growth rate per annum. You'll have to trust me on this, but it means the investor expects three times return on the original investment in five years or less. So if the total investment is five hundred thousand dollars, the investor will expect that the one winner will generate a one-and-a-half million-dollar return. Not knowing which venture will be the ultimate winner means that initially, each investment must have the potential to be the winner."

"Wow! That's incredible," said Jack, impressed with his uncle's financial acumen.

"Now, think about this. Let's say the investor owned twenty percent of the company's stock in exchange for the hundred thousand dollar investment. If the investor's share of the return is one-and-a-half million dollars, the founder's share is six million."

"Wow!" Jack repeated. "How can you calculate all of that so quickly in your head?"

"It's what I do, Jack. I'm an investor. These are the basic principles, concepts and skills I've developed over a lifetime of making and losing money. The keys are discipline, due diligence, and never, ever investing more than you are willing to lose. I invest on the premise that I could lose all of my investment."

Then Max turned the tables. "Here's the $64 million question, Jack."

"$64 million. What does that mean?"

Max took a deep breath and sighed. "Never mind what it means. Google it! Let me re-phrase. The *key* question is, are you okay with the investor getting one-and-a-half million dollars and you getting six million dollars on the premise that you would've gotten nothing without the hundred thousand dollar investment?"

"Yes."

Max smiled, not at Jack's answer but in noticing that Jack pushed the last bite of biscuit into the last bite of cheese grits and loaded them onto his fork. "Liked that ironman breakfast, huh Jack?" Without giving Jack time to answer, Max plowed ahead. "It's good you agree with the investor position. Otherwise, I can tell you your car idea would be dead in the water."

"I get the picture."

"Now that you've scarfed down your breakfast, I'll eat and you talk," said Max, as he cut into a slab of fried ham steak.

"Uncle Max, Liz has already commented on my expanding vocabulary. Wait until I tell her I scarfed down my breakfast today."

"Shut up and talk," said Max, with a wink.

Both men laughed.

For the next ten minutes, Jack shared all the information he had learned over the past week about the various types of investors, the investment process, new terms, investor criteria, and a host of other observations. He explained how he networked into two investor interviews. One connection came from his dad, and the other through a golfing friend. Jack classified one of the investors as very sophisticated and the other as more of a gambler. Max was pleased with the report. He thought his nephew was quite sharp.

Max glanced at his watch and said abruptly, "Geez, I'm late! I have a contract signing downtown. Mildred, we need a check!"

Mildred laid the check on the table next to Max's coffee cup. Max put his middle finger in the middle of the check, twirled it around, and slid it slowly and deliberately to Jack's side of the table. "This one's yours, Jack. No free rides." Jack reached for his wallet just as his cell phone started to vibrate. Picking up Jack's phone and pressing the answer button, Max spoke into the receiver: "Jack's busy. He'll call you back later."

"Uncle Max!" exclaimed Jack, as he laid a twenty-dollar bill on the ticket.

"Keep the change, Mildred," Max told the waitress, who was carrying three full breakfast plates lined up the length of her left arm and a pot of coffee in her right hand.

To Jack, Max said: "Let's walk and talk. Here's your assignment for next week."

Jack took out a small notebook, thinking to himself, *no more scribbling on napkins*!

"Next week, we're going to talk about your opportunity. We're going to start by defining the problem. For your venture to be successful, your product must solve a problem. I want you to identify and document what the problem is, how big it is, why it's a problem, who's working on the problem, and how others are trying to solve it. Any questions?"

"Nope," Jake said quickly, perhaps too quickly. After a pause, he furrowed his brow.

"Let me ask it for you, Jack. You want to know where all of this is leading, right?"

"Well, yes," said Jack, wondering how Max could always be so perceptive.

"Jack, I'm committed to helping you realize your dream, if in fact, it's possible. Today, it's too early to know whether your deal can become a reality. But it gives me a chance to offer you the benefit of my experiences, knowledge, lessons learned, and passion for entrepreneurship. If it doesn't work out this time, it will better prepare you for the next venture opportunity. Either way, I'm committed to giving you all the help and guidance I can, if you're willing to take it. It's called mentorship. However," Max added in a parental tone, "there is one condition."

"What's that?"

"Leave your cell phone in the car," directed Max, with a probing look to assess Jack's reaction. He paused long enough for Jack to consider his answer. "Do we have a deal?"

"We do, Uncle Max. You're the best!"

"Next week then. Same time. Same place."

Chapter 4
The Value Proposition

A light rain was falling as Jack pulled his BMW into the café's gravel parking lot. He sighed as mud splattered the car. He sure wished it were a paved lot. The overnight rain had left big puddles randomly distributed across the uneven pebbles. At six-thirty in the morning, customers had plenty of options for parking. Jack was concerned about the potential damage the conditions fostered for those who would arrive later. Would they knock pebbles onto his car? Would they ding his door? Miscalculate a parking space? Jack maneuvered into a parking spot where he could avoid stepping into an ankle deep pool. When he walked in, Max had his coffee cup to his lips while looking down. The *Wall Street Journal* littered the table.

Seeing Jack, Max peered over the top of his reading glasses, which seemed proportionately small for his head. Max grinned. Jack's wet hair was plastered to his head. "You own a hat, Jack?"

"Morning, Uncle Max," Jack said, as he brushed wet bangs aside. As he did, a few drops of rainwater sullied the journal's stock page.

No sooner had Jack sat down than the cell phone vibrated on his belt. His daily alert from *USA Today* was loading on his Blackberry. "Oh crap!" Jack remembered. "I'm sorry, Uncle Max. I told myself this morning in the shower not to forget to leave the cell in the car, but with the rain and all, I forgot. I'll turn it off."

"No problem, Jack," Max said, with a smile. "So today, we're going to get serious about your car deal. We're going to begin characterizing the importance of your opportunity within the context the problem the car deal will solve. Make sense?"

"Yep."

Max compared the problem and the solution to a mathematical equation. If the product only solves part of the problem, the value of the product is less than one that solves a greater part of the problem. If the product solves part of a *big* problem, it could have a greater value than a product that totally solves a small problem. He closed with the observation that investors are most attracted to products that totally solve truly big and growing problems.

Mildred slid two plates stacked with pancakes, corned beef hash, and two poached eggs in front of each man. "Farmer Brown specials," Mildred explained. "Coffee, Jack?"

Jack looked bewildered.

"I took the liberty of ordering," Max said, with a mischievous grin. "Now as I was saying, the success of your car deal will first depend on what problem it solves. Cars have been around a long time. Even as we speak, every car company in the world is working on producing more fuel efficient and greener cars. So let's start by clarifying the problem. You talk. I hate to eat cold pancakes."

"I hate cold pancakes, too." Jack took a big bite from his stack and began talking with his mouth full. "Uncle Max, here's the main problem as I see it." Jack paused to set the proper stage for his profound discovery. "Cars are expensive." He paused again for the answer to settle in with his uncle. Then he continued. "Cars are expensive because they're an extension of the consumer's personality."

"Hmm, interesting thought. I'm listening."

"The expense of a car is far more than the purchase price. There's environmental expense. There is resource depletion expense. There is social expense. There's human expense." Jack provided facts, figures, and projections on each to back up his observations. More importantly, he provided data on the future implications of these indirect expenses, based on an expanding global market. His conclusions were compelling. Even with improvements in fuel efficiency and emissions, the shear increase in the number of vehicles would do virtually nothing to resolve the big problem. The total expense to the planet, he explained, is growing exponentially while the solution is growing incrementally.

Jack went on to explain that Henry Ford's concept was to make an automobile available to the consumer as a nondescript commodity, one that was available to the common man at an affordable price. As everyone recalls, automobiles came to life with one original style and one color, black. Over time, the automobile became for many a disposable status symbol with a depreciating value. For a few passionate aficionados, it became a collectable. But for the majority of consumers, it reflected aspects of their personality from something as simple as preference in color to more complex considerations, such as lifestyle. Were it not for consumer personalities, one car company could produce three or four fundamental styles, all with the same features, and in one color. If this were the case, the average person would buy two or three vehicles over the period of a lifetime, and mass transit would be far more prevalent.

"The problem is clear and well documented, but it's only being marginally addressed. As you said, Uncle Max, big problems require big solutions. I think I have a solution based on Henry Ford's original value proposition. Give 'em any color they want as long as it's black." Jack sat back in the booth, awaiting Max's response.

"Well, I wouldn't label your problem statement as big. I'd call it gargantuan," Max observed. "The question is whether or not your solution measures up to the magnitude of the problem."

"I think it does. Hear me out. The answer depends as much on changing human behavior as it does changing the technology, but I want to start with the technology. Without the technology, human behavior would never change." Jack sopped up maple syrup with his last bite of pancake.

Jack's involvement with his dad's equipment company had exposed him to the full gambit of transportation technology, engineering, manufacturing, distribution, and sales. He had learned it all, knew it well. He was as comfortable pulling an engine block from a D-9 Bulldozer as he was pitching a million-dollar sales deal to a fleet manager in a state transportation department. Along the way, he had participated in more than a dozen equipment innovation upgrades involving geospatial, solar, nanomaterial, fuel, and engine technologies.

"Uncle Max, I think the technical solution is not that difficult. I can and have built a car that gets one-hundred-and-twenty miles per gallon on sweet sorghum ethanol, has quick acceleration, and can reach seventy miles per hour at cruising speeds," said Jack, reducing his voice to almost a whisper, as if the other three patrons in the café could possibly overhear.

"Holy cow!" Max raised his eyebrows and leaned closer to Jack.

Jack went on to explain that computer simulation analysis by a national testing facility verified his design. The input variables were average performance numbers, which meant the ultimate product would perform at least as good if not better than predicted. The engine, fuel, structural materials and electronics were all innovations with superior performance features. The engine design was virtually frictionless; the structural materials were ten times lighter and stronger than the best materials currently available. The car design was for two people and weighed less than a thousand pounds.

"Uncle Max, at full production the projected material cost for this car is little more than a thousand dollars. With air conditioning, add another hundred-and-fifty."

"Whoa!" Max sat back to soak in the price value proposition. Suddenly, he signaled for Mildred, who was nearby. "Darlin', more coffee please." After watching Mildred head for the coffee pot, Max turned back to Jack. "Sounds very impressive and intriguing initially, but you said it yourself. Cars are an extension of the consumer's personality. We have already seen the American consumer reject the micro style auto. Who's gonna buy your little car?"

"Everyone," Jack said with confidence.

"You know something I don't know?" Max turned to Mildred, who was pouring coffee. "Is this yesterday's coffee?"

"Max, I don't want to hear any of your lip!" snapped Mildred. The tempo of their banter might surprise onlookers, yet they shared a genuine appreciation for each other.

As Mildred turned to walk away, apron strings fluttered behind her like angel wings. Jack began again. "Uncle Max, you know I do a lot of work with the state department of transportation. I also serve on the State Turnpike Authority Board. We get regular reports from Washington on proposed and new legislation. They ask us to provide comments. In the last eighteen months, there has been legislation passed at the state level to gradually convert high occupancy vehicle lanes into fuel efficient HOVs. In other words, only fuel-efficient cars will eventually get access to HOVs. Over time, fifty percent and eventually all highway lanes will be free to fuel-efficient cars while all other vehicles will pay to drive on any road in the United States." Jack paused. "Uncle Max, it's coming."

"I'll be darned. Now it all makes sense. I've always wondered why there was so much emphasis on nationalizing the automotive industry."

Jack nodded. "My strategy is to incentivize the market to change human behavior instead of penalizing it. If I can convince the consumer that it is in their economic *and* personal interest, I can sell them a car."

"Jack, I hear you, but hear me. Investors are extremely reluctant to invest in a deal that requires educating the market on the value of your product."

"I don't think education will be required. This will be a blinding flash of the obvious to the consumer. My fundamental premise is the consumer can have their cake and eat it, too. My concept suggests the consumer will only need one primary vehicle, the one that reflects their personality, and one or more eco-cars." Jack's BMW came to mind. "The eco-car will become the one the consumer uses primarily for commuting or short errands."

Jack was quick to point out that it was his gut feeling that consumers were reluctant to adopt the little car because of image. "It's the 'real men don't drive little cars' and 'Lexus owners don't drive cheap cars' syndrome," he said. "If I can help the consumer realize they look smart driving a little car, or better yet, they look frivolous driving a big car, it will shift perceptions."

"Yeah, but your challenge still requires changing consumer behavior, which still requires education. I'm missing the incentive proposition." Max questioned the logic.

"Here's the answer, Uncle Max. Today, the automotive industry sells by appealing to the consumer's personality, as I said before. They are masters at advertising style, selling power, speed, luxury, price, and freedom of the road. I intend to advertise intelligence, time and money. If you buy my car, you will not find yourself stuck in rush hour traffic. You'll literally save thousands per year. Smart people will recognize the benefits."

Max took a final sip of coffee and gathered up his newspaper, tucking it under his arm. Jack checked his watch. An hour had passed by in a flash. Jack looked out the window and noticed the sky was clearing. Knowing when the customer was finished was second nature to Mildred, who appeared at the table and instinctively placed the check on Jack's side of the table. "Have a good day, gentlemen," she said, as Jack slipped a twenty from his money clip and passed it to Mildred with the ticket.

"Keep the change, Mildred," Jack said, with a growing sense of familiarity toward the waitress. She had, he sensed, served customers for at least a couple of generations.

After she disappeared, Max took over. "Jack, here's where I think we are. You've made a good case on framing the problem statement. It *is* a real problem. It's a big and growing problem. It's one that begs for a solution. You have made a good case on providing a solution to the problem. Your value proposition is clear. Your eco-car will reduce the magnitude of the problem. Your solution is multi-faceted. It has a green element, a social element, and a financial element. You have empirical evidence that your eco-car is technically feasible. You've made a good beginning."

"I hear an assignment coming," Jack said, laughing.

"There will always be assignments," Max reminded him. "Your assignment for next week is critical. I want to see preliminary technical and market validation. Validation is a term you will hear over and over until you are sick of it. You'll soon believe I'm obsessed with validation ... and you'll be right!"

"Uncle Max, I know the definition of validation, but just to be sure we're both on the same sheet of music here, be more specific."

"Here's what I mean. If you say you can produce this car for, say five thousand dollars, I want to see the numbers, and not numbers you have estimated. I want to see quotes from third parties. If you say you can sell ten cars a day, I want to see verified expressions of interest from your target markets who indicate they are willing, capable and interested in buying your car. I want to see their names and telephone numbers. I might even want to chat with them. For the moment, it's enough to get what I call qualitative information or enough representative information that it probably reflects reality."

As the two men got up from the table, Max continued to lay out instructions. He told Jack to identify the features and benefits that would make the car different and unique. He wanted Jack to identify why his car would be better than the competitors' would. Max wanted him to focus on anything protectable by patents or exclusive license agreements. As they walked across the gravel, Max scribbled a list of terms he wanted Jack to understand clearly: intellectual property, patent process, types of patents, license agreements, types of license agreements, and stages of production.

"I also want you to calculate a rough estimate on what it will cost to manufacture your car, and I want you to talk to as many people as you can who are representative of your target market. Ask what they think about your idea. Ask what would motivate them to buy your eco-car. Ask what price they would be willing to pay for it. Ask what price they would *not* pay. I could load you up with a lot more, but this is probably all you can get done between now and next week."

As Max climbed into his SUV, Jack asked, "How long have you been driving this gas-guzzler?"

"Eight years," Max responded unapologetically. "Two more years and I'll trade it in for a new one. I know you are thinking I can afford to drive anything I want, but remember, an automobile is a depreciating asset. I'm not concerned with what other people might think." Then after a pause, he changed direction. "Never mind, I don't have time for that lesson. I'll save that one for another time. Tell your dad to give me a call. I want him to support the Boy Scouts banquet again this year."

"Will do. Same time, same place, next week?"

"Oh, no, no, no … I forgot. I have to be in New York on Wednesday. Let's meet Saturday."

"At six-thirty in the morning?" Jack asked, hoping to hear a different answer.

Max smirked. "Sure. Why not? You'll be home before Liz and the boys wake for breakfast."

"Okay, Saturday it is."

Chapter 5
Venture Validation

Max laughed out loud when Jack entered the café. Wearing cargo shorts, a golf shirt, flip-flops, with dark shades dangling on the end of his nose, Jack looked like he had just rolled out of the sack. "Jack, you want to borrow Mildred's hair brush?" Max teased.

"Geez, this is early. We were out past midnight. I need coffee," Jack said as he slowly slid into the booth.

"Coffee coming up, Jack," Mildred said, as she sat a mug down on the table.

Jack watched the hot coffee pour from Mildred's pot. He wondered where he might buy one of these thick-lipped coffee mugs. He liked the weight of it and the way it sounded when he stirred in his sweetener. It had a mellow alto sound, unlike the soprano tingling of his coffee cups at home. Jack noticed details more than other folks did, which is one reason why he was successful.

"Mildred, Jack had a long night. I think he needs a caliente special with a spicy V8. Make mine the same."

"Two calientes!" Mildred barked to the cook behind the dividing wall.

"Two calientes," the unseen cook echoed back.

With the food ordered, Max got down to business. "Well, did you make any progress, Jack?"

"Sure did. Where do you want me to start?"

"Start with the car estimate."

"The research on intellectual property was enlightening. You know we've licensed in technology before at the company, but I didn't pay much attention to it. I left it up to the lawyers, but I sure know a lot more about it now. You can bet I'll be more informed the next time we do something related to our equipment operation."

"That's good," Max said, nodding. "Investors put tremendous value on intellectual property. The more you have, the more attractive you usually are."

Jack began systematically describing the technical elements of the car. A radical, fuel efficient, new generation combustion engine that would burn biodiesel, ethanol, or gasoline would provide the power. Jack came across it when the inventors approached him about incorporating it into riding lawn mowers at the equipment company. He was very impressed with the engine features and performance data, but had decided against it because his company was only a distributor for the mowers and not the original equipment manufacturer. However, he was sufficiently impressed that he structured an exclusive agreement with them for use in on-road vehicles weighing less than fifteen hundred pounds. The engine's unique features allowed for a much smaller engine block.

Equally important was another one of Jack's discoveries. He had recently made contact with a plastics company that invented a polymer with metallic characteristics. After some lengthy discussions, they were sure they could make a heat resistant engine block that weighed one-third as much as aluminum. He had negotiated an exclusive agreement to use this new material for engine blocks. After thinking about it weeks later, Jack had a "eureka!" moment. *If I can cast an engine block, why not cast all the chassis and body pieces for the car?* His concept was verified. Not only could all of the structural components be cast from the high strength, lightweight material, the car would also be virtually indestructible.

The new car components would completely reconfigure the automotive supply chain. Half of the suppliers would go away and the remaining suppliers would be new. Jack was convinced the facility, equipment, labor, and capital resource allocations to make the car were one-tenth the cost of conventional automotive manufacturing.

"Uncle Jack, even if my calculations are off by fifty percent, my car is still hugely competitive."

"I like what I hear," said Max. "You've got clear and compelling competitive advantages protected with exclusive license agreements. What about your cost estimates?"

After checking half a dozen pockets in his cargo pants, Jack found what he was looking for. "Got 'em right here."

As he was leafing through his pocket notebook, Mildred approached the booth holding a plate in each hand with potholders. "Hot plates, fellas. Two caliente specials."

Jack looked down at the concoction. It started with a corn tortilla on the bottom, stacked with a thick slice of Canadian bacon, another tortilla, two fried eggs covered with melted goat cheese, and all of it topped with a red chili salsa. "Whew, that looks spicy!"

"Dig in. You're gonna love it! Mildred, do you have any Mexican hot sauce?"

Jack picked up his fork and paused for a moment to muster up the courage to try a tiny bite of the salsa. It was hotter with spice than Jack was accustomed to.

"Jack, you don't eat the salsa by itself," Max admonished him. "Get some eggs and tortilla with it. You must not get out very much!"

Both men grinned.

Jack succumbed to the spices and dug in. As he raised a heaping, dripping morsel to his mouth, he lurched forward to catch it and avoid dripping spicy juices down the front of his shirt. After successfully swallowing his first taste, he rested his fork on his plate. Satisfied, he began rattling off the material quotes for each of the car components, along with labor and equipment costs.

It was surprisingly inexpensive, thought Max. He did not doubt Jack's numbers. This is what he did for a living. His job required that he plan, estimate, order, build, deliver, and collect. Max thought to himself, *so far so good.*

"What about potential customers?"

"I started off talking with anyone I came across and got nothing but positive feedback. It was so positive that I began to question my process. I asked myself if they were telling me what I wanted to hear because they wanted to be supportive. So I changed my approach. I scripted a survey. It made the process much more efficient, and I was able to get 22 surveys completed."

Max dabbed salsa from the corner of his mouth with a paper napkin and asked, "Did you reach a conclusion?"

"Yes, I would say fifty percent were strongly favorable, a quarter were favorable, and the balance were all over the page, each with a unique, and what I thought to be realistic reason why the idea would not work for them."

Max quizzed Jack at length on his findings. He asked questions Jack had never considered. Max's rapid-fire queries followed by tentative assumptions and probing observations surprised Jack. Within a short time, Max had led Jack through a process resulting in categories of market segments, demographics and key decision factors. Max was generally pleased with the outcome. There appeared to be preliminary market validation to justify moving the opportunity forward.

Both men, finished with their breakfast, simultaneously slid their empty plates toward the edge of the table for Mildred to retrieve. Max was quiet for a moment. He pinched his pursed lips, a sign he was deep in critical thought. "Here's where we are. We have preliminary technical validation that the product is producible at a competitive price with defendable competitive advantages. We have preliminary market validation that multiple market segments express conditional interest in the product. The next question we must answer is can we make any money with your eco-car."

"Oh, Uncle Max, I am sure of it! I mean if my numbers are right and I think they are, we can make a lot of money!"

Max rested his elbows on the table and his chin on clinched fists. He did not say anything for a long time. "Jack, I think we have a real opportunity in front of us, but here's the deal. We are still a long way from counting any money. It is one thing to know that we have a potential product, market and profit. It's another challenge to identify a venture model that will generate exponential growth and attract investors. And, trust me; this venture will require a lot of private equity as a financing source."

"Do you think it's fundable, Uncle Max?"

"Jack, it's too early to ask that question in spite of your excitement. Be careful not to contract what I call the 3-E syndrome: excessive entrepreneurial enthusiasm."

Jack worked hard to disguise a guilty laugh. "I'll try!"

"Now, Jack, we have just enough information to get ourselves in trouble. You and I are about to blaze a new trail. A toast is in order." Max raised his coffee cup. Jack raised his. "To you, me, and our adventure!"

The coffee cups clanked more than clinked. Nevertheless, caught up in the spirit, Jack responded with "here, here!"

"We're now launching into a new stage of venture development. It's called the feasibility stage. We are going to spend some serious money. We are going to build a working prototype of the eco-car, commission a marketing firm to assist us with market research, and develop an economic feasibility study. I'm not sure what that's likely to cost, but I would guess somewhere in the range of one hundred thousand to five hundred thousand dollars. The question we must answer is, what percentage of ownership is fair to you and me for my capital investment."

"I've been wondering the same thing," said Jack.

"I'll bet you have!" Max laughed knowingly. "Are you afraid I'll want eighty percent of the deal?"

"I know you'll treat me fairly, Uncle Max."

"Jack, from this point forward, I don't want you to think about what's fair. I want you to think about what's good for the business. Understood?"

"Understood."

Max sat quietly for a while, deep in thought and oblivious to everything around him. He didn't even notice when Mildred gave him a refill. "Okay, here's the deal. When a venture is still an idea, it's hard to put a price on it. One way is to compare it to similar deals that other investors have done in our area. Another is to use a national average on the value of all startup deals. However, since you are family, I am going to do it the easiest way I know how. Jack, tell me, would you sell this opportunity lock, stock and barrel today for five hundred thousand dollars?"

"What do you mean?" Jack sounded surprised.

"I mean, if I wrote you a check for five hundred thousand dollars today, would you sign over all your license agreements and walk away?"

"No way. This opportunity could be my once in a lifetime venture!"

"What if I offered you a million dollars?"

"Wow! That's different," Jack said, haltingly. He thought for a second and asked, "Do you have your checkbook with you?"

Max laughed. "That's my boy!" The couple at a nearby table turned to see what was causing such excitement. "Perfect answer. Take the money! Okay, we just set an agreeable value on your opportunity. Today, it is worth one million dollars. That's what you'd take for it, and what I'd be willing to give you for it."

"Cool! I've got a million dollar venture!"

"On paper." Max reminded him. "Now, here's the deal. Our objective is to build a working prototype that we can test and validate its performance. It'll cost somewhere between one hundred thousand and five hundred thousand dollars to do that. I'm prepared to invest up to a half-million. My percentage of equity ownership will be determined by the amount of investment required to finish and test the prototype and the market research. If it costs me the full five hundred thousand dollars, I'll own thirty-three percent of the business. Are you okay with that?"

Jack thought for a minute. "Wouldn't that be fifty percent, Uncle Max? A half million is one half of a million dollars, right?"

"No. The total value of the deal is your original one million dollars, plus my investment of a half-million. That makes a total venture value of $1.5 million. You see?"

"Okay." Jack did not sound very sure of the answer.

"A lot of people make the same mistake. It is fairly common. Now in the event we can get the work done for less than five hundred thousand dollars, my ownership stake will be proportionally less. If it's more, it will be proportionally more. Deal?"

"Deal!"

"You want your attorney to draw up the papers or mine?" asked Max.

"Oh, I'm sure yours will be fine, Uncle Max."

"Wrong answer, Jack. You always have your attorney draw up the papers when possible. That's Lesson 9.

"Lesson 9? Are you kidding me? Are you really keeping count?"

"No, I'm just messing with you! Let's go. Your boys will be waking up soon, and they will want to spend Saturday with their dad. Got plans?"

"Today, it's soccer."

"I'll call you in a few days with your next assignment. I want to mull it over for a while first." Max got up and said, "You get the check. You're the majority stockholder."

Chapter 6
The Business Model

Liz watched the waiter fill her flute with champagne. She always enjoyed watching the bubbly fizz settle into the glass. She associated it with happy occasions and tonight was one of those times, her tenth wedding anniversary. It had been months since she and Jack had been out for a meal. His obsession with the new venture had consumed his every waking moment, except for an hour of quality time with Gray and Noah each evening and soccer on Saturday mornings.

Overall, she felt like he was managing everything well under the circumstances. He had temporarily given up Saturday golf rounds and Wednesday night tennis matches, but still made time for Noah's soccer games and Gray's swimming lessons. But it wasn't unusual to find him poring over designs and spreadsheets in the wee hours of the morning. He assured Liz it would not be this way much longer. Five of the twelve months had passed since they made their agreement. In spite of Jack's hard work, she had never seen him so energized.

Jack raised his glass. "To us!" Liz acknowledged the gesture and both drank from the delicate, crystal flutes.

"This is so nice, Jack. We haven't had an evening out in months, just the two of us."

Jack smiled. He thought how pretty Liz looked in her simple black dress and pearls. She was a classic beauty and had aged gracefully. The pearls reminded him of Hawaii. He had bought them for her birthday on their first vacation to Maui. He sighed. *No vacation this summer. No time to spare.* Nevertheless, they were together, happy and healthy. Overall, they were richly blessed.

"Happy anniversary, sweetheart." Jack whispered to Liz.

Jack and Liz had a sumptuous dinner and lingered over coffee and dessert. Soft music played. Neither one was inclined to leave. They talked about a dozen topics, catching up with each other on the small things that busy professional couples never seem to have time to do. As the restaurant lights went from dim to bright and the cleaning crew began to stack chairs, they reluctantly declared the evening over.

Driving home, Liz asked, "Jack, how's it going with Uncle Max?"

"Liz, you would never believe how much I've learned from that man. It's incredible! He has a mind like a computer. I admire him a lot."

"No kidding," Liz said, chuckling. "I can tell that he's your new hero. I'm envious." She paused for a moment and said, "But tell me how it's really going. You have not mentioned any progress in several weeks. All I see is work, work, and work."

"I hope you don't feel like I'm ignoring you, Liz," Jack said sincerely.

"Honestly, I do, Jack, but I know you're doing the best you can. It does help though when you talk with me about it. It makes me feel like I'm part of it when you keep me in the loop."

"Liz, I love telling you about it, but I get concerned that my excitement may make you think I care more about the venture than I do the family."

"No, Jack. The more you tell me, the better I feel. We are in this together. Anyway, talk to me about it."

Jack began to give her details in a normal tone of voice. Within a couple of minutes, his words were coming rapidly, nearly as fast as he could possibly talk. They had cast five engines with the new design and metallic polymer. The initial performance tests exceeded everyone's expectations, including the computer simulations. They were keeping the results confidential for the time being. The single most important technical milestone was now accomplished. The first eco-car designs and a rough prototype were completed. Some of the body parts and chassis components were made of a variety of materials, with strict attention paid to the weight factors to ensure the prototype testing would be as close as possible to real performance. The road test—the test everyone was waiting for—was scheduled to take place within a few weeks. At that time, they would know the full magnitude of their venture opportunity. "I get so excited at times, I can hardly breathe," Jack said, as they undressed for bed. He had talked nonstop for nearly an hour. Liz slept comfortably that night.

Early Sunday morning, Jack's cell phone vibrated on the night table. "I hope I didn't wake anyone," said Max.

"Just me," grumbled Jack.

"A little grumpy this morning, are we?" Max asked, with a laugh.

"Uncle Max, it's six o'clock in the morning. It's Sunday. I had other plans for the next two hours, like sleeping."

"You'll get over it, Jack," said Max. "I've been awake since two o'clock thinking about our business model. Get up, get a shower, get dressed, get some coffee and then call me. I want your undivided attention for an hour this morning."

Forty-five minutes later, Jack sat down at his desk in the den and dialed Max's number on the house phone. He put the call on speakerphone and waited for Max to answer. Max did not bother with hello. He began immediately. "I've been thinking about our business model off and on for the last two weeks. Something was bugging me, and I just could not find the underlying cause of it. Now, I know what it is. We are not going to sell cars. We're going to sell franchises."

"I'm hearing, but not understanding." Jack was puzzled.

"The grad students in the MBA program did a great job on identifying our potential target market segments and the competitive marketing analysis, but if you remember, they weren't too keen on our distribution strategy. The idea of marketing through established dealerships or even setting up our own is a costly proposition. It requires a national rollout with a huge advertising budget, and then there is our objective to sell a hundred cars in a hundred major markets. Very costly."

"No doubt about it. Is there an alternative?"

Max reiterated the results of the market research once again for his own satisfaction. It pleased him each time he recalled the outcome. The report indicated that rural areas, business commuters, destination resorts, and central business districts were primary markets for the eco-car. The research showed the eco-car was attractive to rural residents for the easy living driving environment, commuters for HOV privileges, resorts for day trips, and downtown workers who take public transportation to work.

"Here's my idea," Max said. "With this model, we can go into three hundred markets with three hundred units. We start with one major market area at a time. We establish one franchise per major market. We set a retail price of ten thousand dollars on the eco-car. Our delivered cost is somewhere around four thousand dollars. We sell the car to the franchisee for six thousand, including tax, title and tags. Are you getting this down?"

"Not so fast, Uncle Max. You said six thousand dollars with tax, title and tags, right? Why not ten thousand?"

"Yes, I said six thousand, because we want the franchisee to understand they're getting a good deal. And they are. The franchisee can lease the car to the customer for one hundred and ninety-nine dollars per month. The franchisee's financed cost is one hundred and twenty-nine dollars per month per car. We collect a franchise fee of forty dollars per month per car, of which ten dollars per car is set aside for advertising, half national and half local. Our minimum order requirement is…"

Even though Jack was writing as fast as he could, it was not fast enough. "Hold on, Uncle Max! What did you say after forty dollars for the franchise fee?"

"I said ten bucks for advertising."

"Uncle Max, before you go further, I need for you to explain to me why we aren't simply selling cars to customers. I'm lost."

"Recurring revenue, Jack," Max explained. "Here's the business model. We offer one franchise per major market. Each franchisee will commit to a minimum of three hundred cars over a five-year period. That's ten cars the first year, thirty the second year, sixty the third year, eighty in year four, and a hundred and twenty cars in year five. We will use the same formula for market penetration. Ten cars in ten markets in the first year, thirty cars in thirty markets in year two, and so on."

Max continued to lay out his plan, and Jack tried his best to absorb it all.

Max's plan was to set up set up one major market every two weeks. His ramp up strategy would require one car per day the first year, easily achievable. Eventually, they would build production capacity to thirty-six thousand cars per year.

"Geez, Uncle Max! This sounds fantastic. But how could we ever build thirty-six thousand cars per year?" Jack's head was spinning with numbers and none of them made much sense.

"First of all, we never will." Max said. "But I'll explain that in a minute. Even if we did, it would be easy. We would produce thirty-six thousand cars in four regional plants, twelve thousand per plant, one thousand per month, two hundred and fifty per week, and fifty per day. With three shifts per day, that's roughly two cars per hour. Very doable. This is a fabulous business model!"

"Uncle Max, I really don't understand this. Why aren't we just making cars and selling them to customers? If our cost is four thousand dollars and our sales price is ten thousand dollars, we net six thousand dollars per unit. That sounds clean and simple to me."

"Jack, you aren't getting it," Max chided. "If you sold one car every hour in an eight-hour day, you'd sell about twenty five hundred cars per year. You would make about ten million dollars per year every year. Not too shabby! But … with my model in the fifth year, we'll net seventy-two million dollars in sales and thirty-two million dollars in franchise fees. We will make thirty-two million dollars every year after that, whether we ever build another car or not. It's all about the power of recurring revenue, Jack."

Max talked about cash flow, distribution channels, national marketing strategies, outsourcing and the supply chain for another twenty minutes. Jack was amazed how Max could take such complex issues and make them seem so simple and achievable. Just then, Jack heard someone rumbling around in the kitchen.

"Hold on a minute, Max. I'm gonna get a refill on my coffee."

"I think I'll do the same. I'm about to lose my voice."

Jack took the phone off speaker mode and walked into the kitchen with the handset. Liz greeted him with a peck on the cheek and asked if Max was on the phone. Jack rolled his eyes with a grin and told her Max was all business this morning.

"Let me have the phone," Liz said, holding out her hand with a fake scowl on her face. Max was back on the line. "Good morning, Uncle Max! How are you?" Max told Liz he was well and thanked her for asking. He apologized for getting Jack out of bed early on a Sunday morning. "Max, what are you doing for lunch?" Hearing he had no plans, she insisted that he come over for pot roast.

"I'll be there," Max answered enthusiastically. "It's been far too long since I've seen you and the boys. Tell Jack we can pick up our chat where we left off after lunch. See you about one o'clock?"

"Yes, that'll be great. See you then."

The boys came stumbling into the kitchen, rubbing their sleepy eyes and looking for cereal bowls.

After lunch, Jack and Max helped Liz clean up the dishes and retired to the den. Liz ushered the boys into the back yard with a soccer ball and asked if she could sit in on their discussion for a while. They insisted.

"I love to hear you guys talk about this new venture. It reminds me of my brothers when we were younger. They were always planning and scheming and getting excited about some new adventure. I always wanted to be part of their plan and they'd usually give me a minor role, like being the look-out."

"If you're not careful, we'll make you the look-out … or maybe the CEO," Max said, with a hearty laugh.

"I don't think a career in interior decorating would qualify me for either one, but I will have a say-so when it comes to picking colors for the new cars," Liz said with modesty.

Both men agreed Liz was on to something. Even though Jack had insisted on one style and one color for the eco-car, he wondered about that aspect of the business plan. For now, Jack wanted to know more about Max's idea.

"Max, I've got more questions than I have answers. Let me ask all my questions and then maybe we can take them one at a time. Okay?"

Max nodded.

"First, why are you so sold on this franchise idea? Second, what did you mean when you said we would never have to sell all the cars? And, third, where will we get all the capital needed to float this deal?"

"Jack, I am sold on the franchise model for a couple of reasons. One is we only have to make three hundred sales, not ten thousand or twenty thousand sales. Each franchise sale represents a minimum of three hundred cars over a five-year period. It is a predicable adoption rate, which is extremely important to us and to investors. It allows us to manage exponential growth with a plan. Another reason is that I have an exciting idea about franchisees."

"What?"

"You're not going to believe this." Max paused to heighten the suspense.

"Tell us!" Liz added, impatiently.

"Grant International Equipment!" Max bellowed.

"Oh, my God!" Liz gasped.

Jack wondered why he had not thought of it himself. "It's perfect!"

How cool was that concept, to have Jack's dad and Max's brother as the company's primary customer? Grant International was located in more than a hundred major markets and had distributorships in several hundred more. Max referred to it as a captured market. They spoke excitedly about what a grand idea it was, and how great it would be to leverage so much business know-how and power.

"I can't wait to tell Dad!" Jack said, giggling like a schoolchild as he moved back and forth across the den.

"Not yet, Jack. We aren't quite ready. But soon. It's time to expand our working group. If you could put together a dream team, who would you recruit as advisors?"

Jack thought for a minute. "For accounting, I'd pick Joshua Barnes, managing director of our accounting firm. I've got legal covered with my attorney, Tom Blake. Wilson Winters, production manager for Haltom Manufacturing, is a good man. That would be it. Oh yeah, Tim O'Brian, he's in charge of marketing for Fleet Leasing Services."

"I like the way you think, Jack," said Max. "Call Roberta and she can set up the meeting. Let's meet in my office.

"And, I want to be there when you pitch Jack's dad on the idea," said Liz, with a twinkle in her eye.

Jack thought to himself that Liz's presence might be a smart move. "One of your pot roasts might butter him up," Jack suggested.

"Your second question," Max continued, "was why we would never sell all the cars." Jack and Liz had all but forgotten the other questions. "The reason is ... we'll be acquired sometime during the fourth year. Our number one objective is to build a company and sell it. If we work our plan, one of the big boys will have to buy us or watch us continue to eat up their market share."

"Your third question was where will all the capital come from? This is a beautiful business model. We will only need one round of investor capital. After that, we'll be able to finance our receivables with short term notes and still throw off a lot of cash flow from operations."

After burning off some nervous energy from pacing, Jack finally sat down. He was amazed at Max's business savvy. He hoped some day that he would know half as much. "I'll make the call to Roberta tomorrow and we'll get this show on the road," he promised Max.

"Sounds like a plan. Let's go see what the boys are up to. I'm gonna have to go soon." It dawned on Max that he had more energy these days. He smiled.

Chapter 7
Murphy's Law

"Mr. Grant, your nephew is holding on line one. If it's okay with you, I'm going to leave a few minutes early and drop off this package at the post office on my way home."

"Thanks, Roberta. Have a good evening. See you tomorrow."

Max picked up the phone. "Hey Jack, what's up?"

"Uncle Max, I've got really bad news. I've tried for two hours to get up the courage to call you." Jack paused. "Max, the test failed."

"What do you mean the test failed? Are you talking about the efficiency test, the emission test, or speed?"

"All of them," Jack answered meekly.

Max took a deep breath, clinched his jaw, and leaned back stiffly in his leather desk chair and sighed. "Geez, that's not good news."

Max and Jack talked for an hour. Max wanted details. Who did the test? When and where was it done? Was Jack there to observe? How many tests did they run? The tests were not that bad compared to existing economy cars, but not good enough to support the business model assumptions. Jack was despondent. It was torturous to answer Max's questions. He asked many of them more than once. All Jack could think about was the time, money, energy, and mostly hope of transforming a great idea into a great product down the drain. Max and Jack agreed to meet at the warehouse on Saturday to review the drawings, look at the data, and see what they might discover. Jack dreaded the three-day wait. He knew it would seem like an eternity.

"Hi, honey," Liz shouted from the kitchen. "You're running late this evening. Dinner's nearly ready. I haven't been home long myself."

"Hi, babe," Jack said flatly. He slumped into his recliner and flicked on the news. He stared at the television without watching. His mind was at the test site. He could see the car going around the track loaded with instrumentation. He reflected back on his frustration each time they completed a trial. *What could it be?*

Liz came looking for him. She knew something was wrong as soon as she saw him. She had never before seen that look, that posture or that stare. "Jack, are you okay?"

"The tests failed today, Liz."

Her heart sank. She did not know what to say. "Do you want to be alone? Can I get you anything?" She had as many questions as Max, but knew he was too raw and wounded to ask. Not now. "I'll let you be alone."

Hours later, Jack got up from the chair. His throat was parched. It had been a long time since he had had something to drink. He retrieved a bottle of water from the fridge and returned to the den. His eyes grew heavier. The next thing he knew, Liz was shaking him awake. It was morning. He had slept through the night in his chair. He forced a smile and a "good morning" to the boys. It was a chore to shower, dress, eat and go to work. Jack could not be more miserable.

Finally, the three longest days of Jack's life passed. He reached the warehouse two hours ahead of Max. He circled the prototype repeatedly. Jack resisted the desire to immediately dismantle it and put it back together again in hopes that something was misassembled.

Max arrived with a short, stocky man. The stranger followed slightly behind Max, with both hands tucked in his pockets.

"Hey Jack, how are you?" Max had a slight tone of forced enthusiasm. "I'll bet you've had a couple of weary days, huh?"

"Oh gosh, you can say that again. Liz told me I should check into the YMCA until I was fit to live with again."

"Are you serious?"

"No, I'm kidding, but she gives me a lot of space."

Max made introductions. "Jack, this is Bill Thompson. He heads up maintenance for my equipment fleet. I invited him to join us. Sometimes another pair of eyes helps."

Bill walked around the car just as Jack had, studying various details.

"Jack, I know you've thought about this for days because I know I have. Do you have any ideas?" asked Max.

Shaking his head and rubbing his brow as if he had a severe headache, Jack admitted, "Not a clue."

"I think we have to work through this systematically, starting with the engine. Why don't you pull out the design drawings?" suggested Max.

"You guys can look at all the drawings you want, but you won't find any answers. Until you properly inflate these tires, you'll never know how this vehicle will perform."

"I'm sorry," said Jack, leaning closer to Bill. "What did you just say?"

"Jack, he said 'air up the damn tires!'" Max shouted with glee. *Could the solution be so simple?* As Max and Jack both realized that yes, it could, Max clapped his hands and shouted again near the top of his voice, "Bill, you are the man!"

Bill explained the small tires had such small depth that it was impossible to look at them and know whether they were properly inflated. He showed them how pushing down on the bumper created little reaction. "You inflate the tires properly and this little car will bounce like a basketball."

"How did you know?" asked Jack.

"These are very similar to the tires we run on our Georgia Buggies. If the tires are underinflated, they will not carry the load. We have to check them every time the weather changes."

Max explained to Jack that a Georgia Buggy was a motorized piece of equipment for transporting concrete. *A wheelbarrow with a motor*, imagined Jack. *How about that!*

"Bill, I'm giving you a new assignment. I need you here from now on," instructed Max.

"Whatever you say, boss."

Jack could feel the weight of the world lift from his shoulders. His energy returned instantly. Soon he was on his cell setting up new test trials. It was going to cost another chunk of money, but he was anxious to spend it. After reaching answering machines with each call, he remembered it was Saturday. The last call was to Liz. "Get a sitter for the boys. We're going out for dinner tonight." She needed no explanation why.

Back at the track a week later, Jack and Max watched the eco-car make monotonous trips around the oval. It was anything but dull. Checking trial data at regular intervals, they were encouraged but not elated with the performance. Jack made a comment about the disappointing performance, to which Bill answered with a ten-minute discourse on weight distribution, momentum, inertia, aerodynamics, and a variety of engineering related observations. Bill continued talking to himself, to anyone who would listen, and to no one in particular.

Jack leaned over to Max and asked in a low voice, "Where did you get this guy?"

"Oh, don't worry about Bill," Max said in a normal tone, much to Jack's discomfort. "He's a little crazy and goes on like this all the time, but he *is* a genius. Plus, he has a master's in mechanical engineering."

"Are you serious? Why would someone with a master's degree in mechanical engineering be an equipment maintenance manager?"

"Because I require all my management people to have advanced degrees, but mostly because he loves equipment, he loves tools, and he even loves grease."

Max turned to Bill. "Hey Bill, are you gonna get us the performance we need out of this buggy?"

"I'll get you there," Bill promised, adding, "It only takes time and money."

Three more weeks passed. Bill had the car built and rebuilt, tested and retested. Each incremental change gradually improved performance until it crossed what Max called the threshold of differentiation. Max had explained that the car must be so sufficiently different from the competition that it is in a class by itself. Moreover, it would have to demonstrate such compelling economic advantages that a consumer would have to discover reasons *not* to buy versus reasons *why* to buy. The eco-car could now get three hundred percent better fuel mileage, fifty percent better acceleration, and equal top speeds compared to the car's closest competitor. Now the issues to conquer were style points. It was time to package the product. Wrap a skin around it.

Back home, Jack began to notice automotive magazines piling up around the den at a faster rate. "Liz, tell me what's going on with the car magazines. They're everywhere. New ones every day."

"I'm looking at body styles, colors, and interiors," Liz explained.

"Well, babe, I don't want to disappoint you, but that's all been worked out. We intend to keep it simple. Black paint and black fabric interior. These little buggies don't even have electric windows or locks."

"Are you sure that's a good idea?"

"Yes, it's an image thing. We want everything about the eco-car brand to signal economic, nothing frivolous, inexpensive, efficient, prudent, and ..."

"And boring!" snapped Liz. "Is this your idea or Max's?"

"Well, I guess it's both our ideas. We agree on this."

"Well, let me say one thing. Max still wears laced-up winged-tip Florshiems. He probably has thirty suits, each a pinstripe in some shade of gray, blue or black. I will bet every shirt he owns is white. And you! You still wear brown socks with black slacks. What do you two guys know about style?"

Liz was on a roll. "And furthermore, does it cost anymore to paint a car blue than it does black?"

"Probably not." Jack smiled. He was fascinated with Liz's engagement with the subject. Then it hit him.

"You're hired, Liz! You're our new designer."

"Good decision," Liz said, assuming Jack was joking.

"I'm serious!"

Liz paused. She studied Jack's face to see if his countenance verified his words. She quickly concluded that he was serious. "Oh Jack! Do you think I could do it?"

"Hell, if I can build a car, you can certainly design one!"

Liz launched into a plan and the roles were suddenly reversed. She was the exuberant one, starting a new sentence before finishing the last one, showing Jack page after dog-eared page in a dozen magazines.

Within an hour, Liz had a plan. She would contact her mentor at the art school. She remembered one of her best friends was a member of the Industrial Design Society. She could set up focus groups. Ideas continued to flow for the remainder of the evening. Jack was exhausted and went to bed. Liz remained awake until the wee hours of the morning.

Early the next morning, Roberta called Jack on his cell phone to remind him of the dream team meeting at Max's office that afternoon. Jack cleared the breakfast dishes from the table. "Get your sweaters, boys. Time to go!" Jack was now alternating with Liz to get the boys to school. She was very organized and making great progress on the style features. She had very interesting results from focus groups representing each market segment. The industrial designer was a godsend with amazing industry contacts. Between her contacts and Jack's in the heavy equipment supply chain, the package came together swiftly.

The dream team arrived for the meeting within ten minutes of each other. One by one, they gathered around Max's small conference table and went to work. Each person knew his role. Max was always sensitive not to take charge or even to give the appearance of leading a meeting. It was clear to everyone that Jack was the leader. The business plan was coming together. Only one piece was missing: a preliminary commitment from the franchisee. Once the franchisee committed, they would be investor ready.

Everyone agreed the next step was critical. John Grant would not be an easy sale. In fact, the family connection would probably make it even more difficult, because he would never allow himself to be in a position where business could sour a family relationship. The team worked for several hours laying out their presentation. They were finally satisfied.

Jack summarized the objective. "What we have to keep in mind is Dad's obsession with risk. For him, risk is acceptable as long as the corresponding reward is proportional. I am confident we can make a best-case argument that the risk-reward model is potentially exponential, and in the worst case, we can offer an attractive abort strategy. We only have one chance to get it right. Dad will listen, and then he'll decide. We'll have his answer at the end of the meeting. Max, can you have Roberta arrange the time?"

"Consider it done."

The meeting with Grant International a week later lasted longer than expected. Scheduled for two hours, it dragged on for four. As expected,

John Grant had tough probing questions. Jack did a masterful job pitching the deal to his father. He anticipated and answered most questions before they were asked. It was a fascinating experience for the dream team. They were like spectators at a prizefight. The discussion began like two men shadowboxing, not throwing any hard punches, asking easy questions, offering simple explanations.

Within minutes, the discussion evolved into a flurry of power punches, none of which could knock out their opponent. It was John Grant's way of challenging his son's confidence in his assumptions. As quickly as the flurry had begun, it was over. The fight was a draw. John Grant was convinced of Jack's confidence and his argument. Then the fight became a waltz. It was a decision making process between father and son that dated back to a time when Jack was barely out of diapers. The team members were finally invited to participate. John Grant listened intently. He decided. He was in.

After the meeting, Jack got into his car with the newest member of the dream team. They hugged and drove home as giddy as two teens.

Chapter 8
The Investor Presentation

Ten months had passed since Liz and Jack agreed to give it a year. They were on schedule, or at least close. The design drawings for the final product were finished and looked fantastic. Liz had done a superb job. The brand was new and exciting. It resonated around concepts of nature and green products. Thankfully, Volkswagen had never protected the term "bug." So the eco-car was now known simply "The Buggy." No one would have guessed that it originated from Bill's tire solution with the Georgia Buggies. After that scare, Bill continued to refer to the car as the buggy and the name stuck.

Liz and the design team came up with clever color themes like bumblebee, ladybug, grasshopper, butterfly, and spider. Each car had a corresponding iridescent metallic paint theme and colorful interior. With each car burning ethanol made from sweet sorghum, the brand had a strong connotation with nature. The mockups looked great. It would be a field day for the marketing and advertising team.

Jack and Bill were logging long hours. Jack's were a result of working his day job first; Bill's was a result of his love for it all. They were close to having a replica of what the final product would look like. Max said investors would probably only fund the venture if they could see and touch the car. Built to scale and specification except for the fiberglass body and aluminum chassis, it was a costly and time-consuming effort. They were amazed at how many heavy equipment components were integrated into the little buggy. The seats from Grant International's 18-ton crane made a luxurious addition. The dash and wiring harness from the front end loader snapped right in place.

As Bill reached for a socket wrench, he told Jack, "You know, no one else will ever realize it, but this little buggy is nothing more than a composite of ten big pieces of road equipment squeezed into a tiny little package."

Jack thought about it and added, "except for the chassis, skin, engine and tires, I think everything has come out of our parts inventory or at least from one of our suppliers. If nothing else, we could sell this car as a kit over the internet."

"Now that's a thought!" The two shared a good laugh.

That evening, Jack called Max. "Uncle Max, it's time to circle the wagons. I think we're ready to pull the trigger on getting in front of investors."

"If you say so. I'll have Roberta get the team together." Max was pleased with the way the control momentum had shifted with the team from him to Jack.

"What do you say we meet at the café tomorrow morning? It's been nearly three months since our last breakfast."

"See you there."

As Max pulled into the parking lot, he noticed Jack's car parked close to the front door. It was the first time Jack had arrived before him. Max found Jack at their usual table, but Jack was sitting on what had traditionally been Max's side of the booth. The men greeted each other and Mildred gave them both some grief for being away for so long. In rhythm, Max ordered the farmer's breakfast; Jack ordered the ironworker's special.

Jack launched into an update on where the project stood. "Max, the prototype will be finished by the end of next week. We have outstanding performance data, a lock on the franchisee, strong market validation from each market segment, an exciting business model, and a good handle on our costs and breakeven analysis. I think we're ready to present to investors. Do you?" Jack felt a tremble of nervous excitement.

Max seemed distracted, flipping through the tabletop jukebox pages. When Max said, "Close, but not quite," Jack's heart skipped a beat. Turning his attention solely to music, Max said, "You know, I'm gonna play a tune. I've been coming here for decades and never played one." Max nonchalantly dropped in a quarter and punched the keys for "Beyond the Sea" by Bobby Darin.

Then Max turned back to Jack. "We still have work to do."

"Like what?"

Before Max could answer, Mildred sat down old-timey soda glasses in front of each man. The pink mixture filling the glass looked like a strawberry shake.

"What that heck is this, Mildred?" Max asked.

"It's your breakfast," Mildred coolly responded.

"No, Mildred," Max gently reminded her. "I ordered a farmer's breakfast and Jack ordered the ironworker's special."

"Max, this is a strawberry smoothie. I ordered it for you," Jack admitted.

"What are you talking about? When did you do this?" Max feigned confusion. He had figured out the answer, but wanted to give Jack a hard time.

"Max, I need for you to be healthier. We have a long, hard row to hoe in front of us. I do not want you running out of gas. I made a point to get here early and give Mildred the recipe. I told her that regardless of what we ordered for breakfast, she was to bring us two smoothies."

"You are so sneaky!" Even though he didn't say so, Max was impressed with Jack's assertiveness. After sticking a spoon in the glass and swirling around the creamy mixture, Max asked, "What's in this thing?"

Jack laughed. "Don't ask. Just drink it. You have made me eat 'heart attack' food for months. Now it's my turn to reverse the tables."

"I am *not* drinking this until I know what's in it." Max crossed his arms like a defiant toddler.

Jack took a deep breath to relax. "Okay, I'm gonna tell you. You are not going to like it, but you are still going to drink it. It has yogurt, powered whey, apple juice, and frozen strawberries."

Max looked up at Mildred. She seemed to be enjoying this scene perhaps more than she should.

"He brought all the ingredients with him," Mildred said. "The only thing we serve that's in that thing is the apple juice."

Jack took a big gulp. "Yum, yum. Drink up, Uncle Max."

Max took a sip. He thought to himself, *this is pretty darn good. Now what do I say without admitting I like it?* He faked an ugly face that connoted displeasure. "Okay, I'll drink this thing, but it's my last one. From now on, you order your breakfast and I'll order mine."

Max took another swallow. "Before you pulled your stunt, you asked me if we're investor ready. We still have some critical thinking and planning in front of us."

Max had a mental checklist of things to do. First on his list was developing a valuation and the offering. Second was developing an investor presentation, and third was strategizing how to manage the investors.

Max explained the process on generating a valuation and offering. The accountant and the lawyer were critical to the effort. He explained the difference between pre-money and post-money valuation. He breezed through a litany of terms that referred to investor and founder's rights and responsibilities. He mentioned due-diligence documentation. Jack, once again, was overwhelmed but confident he would pick it up. Max was a good teacher.

The presentation format was straightforward—a twenty- to thirty-minute presentation supported by video clips, PowerPoint, printouts, and Liz's mockups. The location would be John Grant's boardroom to demonstrate the full force of Grant International's support. Plus, the investors could step outside and see the prototype.

"In fact, we'll have an unveiling. Let the investors be the first outsiders to see it!" Max had a great sense of self-satisfaction at coming up with another fine idea. "We'll have a champagne toast. Make them feel like they're already part of the team."

Max turned serious again. "We've got to get a lead investor, one who can bring others on board. We'll need to figure out who it is and give him a personal presentation, and then let him help us bring the right investor group to the table," said Max, thinking aloud. "I have a couple of folks in mind."

Jack had worked with the dream team through three intense sessions. In between, he educated himself on everything he could learn about valuations, term sheets, private equity, and investor preferences, criteria, and expectations. Each meeting achieved the intended outcomes. They were soon ready with their offering and their presentation. The next objective was meeting with a lead investor.

When Jack was back at home watching the late evening news, the phone rang. Liz wondered who would be calling so late. It was Max. He needed to speak with Jack right away. Liz was concerned about the sense of urgency in his voice.

"Meet me at the café in the morning. We have an investor meeting," Max said with excitement.

"At the cafe?"

"Yes. We have thirty minutes with Simon Jones. We ran into each other at a bank board meeting, and he told me he was looking to place some money. I gave him an elevator pitch. He wants to meet you."

"Have you called the rest of the team?"

"No. This is just you and me."

Max and Jack each only ordered coffee. Neither was particularly hungry. Mildred thought it was odd. Simon Jones walked in exactly at the appointed time. He looked like a cowboy going to church wearing faded jeans, cowboy boots, and a corduroy sports coat. Yet he wore it with a moneyed confidence that worked well for him. Max made introductions. Simon Jones explained he was short on time due to another appointment. Jack had barely started his pitch before Simon Jones asked him several questions about his background that did not seem very relevant. He continued to explain the opportunity with what seemed like constant interruptions. At last, Simon Jones indicated he had to go.

"Let me know when you want to meet. I'll bring a couple of my buddies," he drawled. Simon Jones was in such a hurry that he was nearly out the door before Max and Jack could thank him for his time and interest.

"What was that all about?"

"Sizing you up," Max explained. "You passed his test."

"What test was that?"

Max explained that Jack might never know what criteria Simon Jones used, but he passed the first test—discovering whether this was a real deal with a capable entrepreneur. He could rest assured that Simon Jones had arrived prepared, and had probably made some calls during the intervening time between his chance encounter with Max and the breakfast meeting.

"Let's order. Suddenly I am starving. Mildred, two caliente specials," shouted Jack.

Max laughed heartily.

Two weeks passed and the investor meeting was on the calendar for two o'clock in the afternoon. Seven high net worth investors had agreed to come. Simon Jones was bringing two of his investor buddies. Jack's dad had invited a golfing pal. Max had asked along an old college friend, who had invited a woman that managed a family investment trust. The seventh investor was an entrepreneur, one of Liz's friends who had recently sold her medical device company.

The investors gathered around the conference table. They were a mixed lot, some in jeans, and some in suits. They represented a wide age range. The dream team sat in chairs away from the table and at the opposite end of the room from the projector screen. Jack launched into the presentation. It was flawless; the words came naturally. Jack communicated with confidence; he spoke convincingly. Max caught Liz's eye and winked. She smiled knowingly. After Jack finished his presentation, he entertained questions for another thirty minutes. When it appeared the questions were over, he invited the attendees to join him in the warehouse to unveil the Grant Motor Company's new Buggy.

Simon Jones interrupted with a request. "Jack, would you and your team give us a couple of minutes? We'll catch up with you in the warehouse."

After leading the team out of the conference room, Jack asked the dream members to go ahead, adding, "We'll be along in a minute." Catching Max by the arm, Jack asked quietly, "What's this all about?"

"They're going into caucus. They will get a sense from each other what their individual thoughts are. What they like. What they don't like," Max explained.

A half hour passed before the investors emerged from the conference room. The two who had accompanied Simon Jones excused themselves, stating they had other meetings to make.

Simon Jones approached Jack and asked if he could have a moment alone with him and Max. The rest of the attendees made their way to the warehouse to see the Buggy.

Once the trio was alone, Simon Jones did not waste time. "I'll be candid. You made a compelling presentation. You have some attractive competitive advantages and a clever business model. But I can tell you there has never been a perfect deal. If there were perfect deals, there would be no need for investors. In summary, I can tell you this decision boils down to the same five risk factors that investors make in every investment decision."

Simon Jones started with the product risk and explained that the big corporations could easily undermine the business strategy by introducing a competitive product and virtually give it away if need be to collapse their little company. Looking at the market risk, he commented that the emerging global economies were already moving into the micro automotive space, and formidable opponents could quickly emerge in spite of their green brand. The management risk was not quite as worrisome due to the depth and breath of the advisors and Jack's experience with equipment production and sales.

Good point, Jack thought to himself. However, the feeling quickly passed when Simon Jones observed that it did not go unnoticed that none of them had ever produced and sold an automobile. The perceived financial risk focused on whether the company was actually asking for enough money to finance the venture. The investors were comfortable with a six million dollar pre-money valuation, but felt like one-and-a-half million dollars might not be sufficient capital, based on the objective of only needing to raise one round. Finally, the investors had noted the execution risk. Given the recent government involvement in the automotive industry, it was not clear whether the government would perceive the new little company as unwanted competition and a challenge to the social good. If the government wanted to, it could make their life miserable.

Jack kept looking at Max during the debriefing to see if he could get a read on Max's reaction. He got none.

Finally, Simon Jones drawled, "Well, let's have a look at your Buggy."

The three men walked toward the warehouse in silence except for some occasional and somewhat awkward chitchat. Along the way, Jack's mind was spinning. *Did Simon give him an answer?* He was not sure. *Did they like the deal?* He did not know.

They gave Liz the honor of unveiling the Buggy. She grabbed the tarp and gave it a quick pull. There it was—a Ladybug version of the Buggy. It was beautiful. Everyone oohed and awed. Jack put an arm around Liz's shoulder, lifted a glass of champagne, looked across at Max, smiled and said, "To the future!"

Everyone echoed, "To the future!"

Simon Jones strolled over to Jack, handed his empty glass to Liz, firmly shook Jack's hand, thanked him for the presentation, and said the magic words: "I'll call you in a few days."

THE END

Venture Acceleration

I n v e n t i o n
I n n o v a t i o n
E n t e r p r i s e

By

H. Randall Goldsmith, PhD

www.venturecapitaltools.com

Introduction

Personal traits usually determine winners and losers among
entrepreneurs – open-mindedness, decisiveness, persuasiveness and the
ability to take setbacks and rejection. For potential entrepreneurs who have

never traveled this path, the following are my guiding principles for commercialization:

Don't bother, *if* ...

You intend to manage your business opportunity to success, rather than relentlessly chase your vision to reality;

Your primary objective is *not* to make a profit;

You are not prepared to devote all of your time and energy to commercialize your venture;

Your family has not given you permission to temporarily neglect them while you commercialize your venture;

You cannot cope with failure;

You are infatuated with your product; or

You are not prepared to lose serious money.

On the other hand, *if* ...

You have exhausted every ounce of your energy and can reach deep inside your spirit for one more drop;

You hit seemingly insurmountable barriers and not only persevere but overcome them;

You can get it all done without misplacing your priorities and sacrificing your values;

You can allow yourself to fall in failure and then get up, dust off and begin again and again;

You are willing to release your grip and give up control to achieve your objectives; and

You are determined to win.

… then you have the right stuff to join the rank of individuals called entrepreneurs.

Good luck!
H. Randall Goldsmith, PhD

Commercialization
The Process of Turning Innovations into Enterprises

There is no doubt—taking a product from concept to market requires skill, resources, and a good deal of luck. A solid commercialization plan will minimize the risk for mistakes and maximize the chances for success. Most agree that you need a road map to direct you through the commercialization process. This is true, but you also need a compass, a survival kit, and plenty of reserve fuel. The journey may start on the interstate, but you will most likely encounter unforeseen roadblocks—obstructions that quickly detour you off the smooth pavement and into the thickets, briar patches and unreliable terrain of a cross-country adventure. Steadfast focus and reliable navigation tools become essential.

It is important to remember that the commercialization environment is dynamic. Even in the best of times, the product that looked *hot* when you started the process may have *cooled* substantially due to new competing technology, a downturn in the economy, unexpected production costs or a hundred other factors. Dead and wounded startups, early-stage, and even mature companies litter the landscape in the aftermath of the dot-com implosion, 9/11, and shaky business climates. Flexibility, quickness, and real time information are vital to success. A solid, strategic plan helps you identify objectives and keeps you moving forward.

The Venture Commercialization Model is a specific set of tools designed to strategically guide your plans and actions for developing a new business. The model breaks down the process into a sequence of three major phases, six key stages, eighteen significant steps and dozens of critical activities that maximize the probability for success. Each phase has technical, marketing and business activities that *must be considered* as you move through the process. The model is a framework designed to help you develop progress measures, identify information and technical assistance needs, project development costs, and forecast financing requirements.

Too often, inexperienced innovators focus on accomplishing all of the technical steps, up to and even including production, before addressing critical marketing and business considerations. Others obtain a patent without market justification or structure business arrangements without calculating the future value of the company. Commercialization is difficult enough, even without missteps and missed steps. While the commercialization process model does not provide the answers, it leads you to ask the right questions like, *how do I get there from here?*

The Venture Commercialization Model was inspired by previous work done by the Department of Energy and Mohawk Research Incorporated's Innovation Process Model and the National Society of Professional Engineers' Cooperative Agreement with the National Institute of Standards and Technology, and further advanced through engagements with technology commercialization centers throughout the United States and Europe.

While presented as a step-by-step model, few things in the real world are ever accomplished in such simplistic fashion. Nevertheless, the following phases, stages, steps, and activities are presented to offer just that – a simplistic model. Each case, as it was in the beginning and will be at the end of the day, will be unique. Some steps are likely to occur before others; some will be completed more easily than others, and a few will be completely skipped or deleted. Simply follow the model sequentially by addressing the technical, market and business activities of each stage before moving to the next one.

Now, consider a few words of caution about using any models or guidelines for commercializing products or ventures. First, simply achieving all the milestones in the steps and stages of this or any other model will not guarantee success. Second, as with any project, two or more heads are often better than one (seek experienced help), and third, be realistic about the process. And never forget, the commercialization process is all about money. Innovators are putting either their own funds or their investors' money to work. The objective is to commercialize a product or venture that will generate a sufficiently attractive rate of return to justify the effort. So consider the practicality of implementing this commercialization model from the financial perspective by posing this question: *where do entrepreneurs get their funding*? Many entrepreneurs would answer, "Anywhere they can!"

Know this: It is difficult for any start-up company to get capital, period. The first thing an innovator learns is that no one will fund an idea. The old saying that ideas are a dime a dozen is almost correct. Research shows there are approximately three thousand ideas for one successful commercial outcome. Practitioners in the commercialization arena assume there are no new ideas under the sun. They often assume if an innovator has an evolutionary idea that five others somewhere in the world have had the same idea. The important aspect lies in the answer to this question: *who has the resources and the ability to get an idea to market?* So, for those who think they should own fifty percent of a company because it was their idea, think again! Lower your sights and be happy with one-half of one percent!

Assessing the Venture Idea

The following paragraph from *The Gilded Age* by Mark Twain and Charles Dudley Warner describes a business plan written by Twain's fictional character, Col. Beriah Sellers. The authors wrote, *"Colonel's tongue was a magician's wand that turned dried apples into figs and water into wine as easily as it could turn a hovel into a palace and present poverty into imminent future riches."*

"I've been experimenting (to pass away the time) on a little preparation for curing sore eyes – a kind of decoction nine-tenths water and the other tenth drugs that don't cost more than a dollar a barrel; I'm still experimenting; there's one ingredient wanted to perfect the thing, and somehow I can't just manage to hit upon the thing that's necessary, and I don't dare talk with a chemist, of course. But I'm progressing, and before many weeks I wager the country will ring with the fame of Beriah Sellers' Infallible Imperial Oriental Optic Liniment and Salvation for Sore Eyes – the Medical Wonder of the Age! Small bottles fifty cents, large ones a dollar. Average cost, five and seven cents for the two sizes. The first year sell, say, ten thousand bottles in Missouri, seven thousand in Iowa, three thousand in Arkansas, four thousand in Kentucky, six thousand in Illinois, and say twenty-five thousand in the rest of the country. Total, fifty-five thousand bottles; profit clear of all expenses, twenty thousand dollars at the very lowest calculation. All the capital needed to manufacture the first two

thousand bottles – say a hundred and fifty dollars – then the money would begin to flow in. The second year, sales would reach 200,000 bottles – clear profit, say $75,000 – and in the meantime the great factory would be building in St. Louis, to cost, say, $100,000. The third year we could easily sell 1,000,000 bottles in the United States – profit at least $350,000 – and then it would begin to be time to turn our attention toward the real idea of the business."

As fantastic as this plan may be, it is even more astounding that similar fantasy permeates business plans even today. It is not unusual to see an entrepreneur pursue financing for a venture with a business plan based upon indefensible assumptions, non-validated technology, and spreadsheet creep. Sophisticated investors are never enticed by this type of plan, even when the entrepreneur is totally convinced of its merits and committed to its success.

So what does an innovator do with an idea for a new product or service? Where does the innovator go from here? There are so many things to consider. What is the best way to get the product to market? How much money will it take? Where will I find investors? First things first.

Concept Phase

The first commercialization activity begins with recognizing a market opportunity. An entrepreneur recognizes a need in the market and knows how to meet it with a new product or service, or an entrepreneur develops a product or service and recognizes a new market application for it. Exploring the technical, market, and business potential and requirements necessary to make the idea a reality is called the Concept Phase. From a funding perspective, this phase is called the "pre-seed money phase," which means entrepreneurs must depend upon their own resources to accomplish this portion of the commercialization process.

The Concept Phase consists of two stages – the Investigation Stage and the Feasibility Stage (see chart above). The Investigation Stage usually involves collecting qualitative information from a variety of sources such as trade magazines, personal interviews, and online research. The primary objective is to gather enough data and information to verify whether the initial idea has sufficient merit to justify moving to the Feasibility Stage. The objective of the Feasibility Stage is to gather sufficient quantitative data to financially model the business opportunity as accurately as possible.

Investigation Stage

First is the Investigation Stage to determine whether there is sufficient market demand to justify pursuing the idea; whether someone else's patent or copyright protects the proposed product, and whether the opportunity is sufficiently viable to support the introduction of a product to the market or sufficient to support a new enterprise. This stage of the commercial development is typically funded by the individual and is relatively inexpensive, usually less than five thousand dollars. It is important to remember at this stage … *if the entrepreneur develops weak assumptions to support wishful thinking, he (or she) is setting himself up for failure.* There are three steps to the Investigation Stage: Technical Concept Analysis, Market Needs Assessment, and Venture Assessment.

Step 1. Technical Concept Analysis.

The first activity to testing these new venture assumptions is to investigate the technical validity of the product. This step is called the Technical Concept Analysis. To have commercial value, the product or service should solve a real world problem better, cheaper, or faster than existing solutions, and the feature advantages of the new product must be powerfully better than existing ones. Entrepreneurs should remember that huge advertising budgets, aggressive marketing strategies, and fierce customer loyalty often support existing products and services. It is seldom enough for an incremental improvement in a product to displace a well-entrenched product already in the market. Also, remember that product benefits take precedence over product features. Customers buy electric drills to make holes, not to get fancy cases.

The next activity is to assess the intellectual property status of any technology involved in the product. This involves determining whether the product or any of its components are covered by intellectual property protection, such as patents or copyrights. If intellectual property protection is in place, then it could signal the need to enter into a license agreement with the previous inventor for rights to use the technology. If there is no intellectual property protection, it could mean the entrepreneur should consider filing a patent or copyright, but not just yet.

A final activity is to discuss the features and functionality of the product with experts who are knowledgeable about the science, engineering, and manufacturability of the product. One might discover that others have tried and failed at exactly the same opportunity, or there is a fundamental flaw in concept, design or other assumptions.

Step 2. Market Needs Assessment.

Assuming all things are still positive, the next step is to investigate a marketing concept for the product. This step is called the Market Needs Assessment. The questions are straightforward and simple: Who will buy the product, how many will they buy, and how much will they pay? Discovering this information is not as simple as asking the questions. At this level of analysis, the information comes primarily from secondary sources such as trade journals, periodicals, existing market studies and electronic data. The permissible margin for error at this level is large. This activity is designed more to qualify the market opportunity than to quantify it at this point in the process. The purpose here is to develop a level of confidence about the marketability of the product.

Step 3. Venture Assessment.

When the market assessment is completed, the entrepreneur is convinced the product can be made, and there is sufficient market demand to justify production, the final step of the Investigation Stage is the Venture Assessment. This step initially involves answering a series of questions in logical sequence: Does it make more sense to license this product opportunity to a company that can take it to market, or does the entrepreneur have the resources and ability to pursue a commercial venture? If the answer is "yes" to licensing, the next questions are: Who are the potential licensees, how much additional development work is required to secure a license, and what are the standard license fees and royalty rates in the industry? If, on the other hand, the entrepreneur decides to pursue a venture, the next questions are: What experts are needed, how much and what kind of capital is required, and what role will the founder play in the venture? The ultimate question, however, is: Will this venture opportunity generate sufficient return on investment to justify the risk?

Once these steps are completed, there is one more action to accomplish – making decisions. If the investigation suggests that this product or service may be too costly to bring to market, does not meet a defined market need, will not generate sufficient revenues to support the business, or any of dozens of other problematic conclusions, stop and go no farther until the problems are resolved – or abandon the idea. If all the information and conclusions strongly support a go forward decision, the entrepreneur is ready to move from a somewhat qualitative investigation to a more quantifiable economic feasibility study. The Investigation Stage is designed to confirm your personal assumptions and intuition about the business opportunity.

Feasibility Stage

The next level of activity in the Concept Phase is the Feasibility Stage. The purpose of this effort is to determine the economic feasibility of the opportunity. There are three steps in the Feasibility Stage: Technical Feasibility, Market Study and Business Feasibility. During this stage, the individual quantifies the market opportunity by identifying the target market, the size of the market, and the appetite of the market for the product. Also during this stage, a model or crude prototype of the product is developed, and a financial model is generated to determine the potential return on investment. Again, accurate assumptions about costs, market potential, and capital requirements are critical. Failure to get solid supporting data, facts, and information about your venture opportunity at this stage makes a risky proposition riskier. Moving forward on a faulty feasibility is self-delusional. Will Rogers said, "The first thing you should do when you find yourself in a hole is to stop digging."

Since this stage requires a more rigorous approach to data collection and analysis and interaction with service providers such as market researchers, patent attorneys, accountants, and industry representatives, this stage is more costly than the Investigation Stage. The ten thousand dollars to fifty thousand dollars in costs occurring in this stage are self-funded with the help of friends, acquaintances, and relatives.

Like every stage in the model, the Feasibility Stage has technical, market and business dimensions, and each should be explored sequentially beginning with technical feasibility followed by market feasibility and ending with business feasibility. Each step should be viewed as a "go/no-go" decision point. As the commercialization process progresses, each step will become increasingly more costly and involve more outside resources and experts. Since the Feasibility Stage is usually self-financed, it is important to move efficiently and effectively through the process in a timely manner.

The feasibility step is very critical. This is the time to be certain you are thorough in investigating all aspects of the opportunity. Failure to do a good job here may well result in the ultimate demise of the product or venture.

Step 4. Technical Feasibility.

The first step, Technical Feasibility, involves the development of a working model of your product or service. It is not necessary for the initial materials and components of the working model to represent those that actually will be used in the finished product or service. The purpose of the working model is to demonstrate, to your own satisfaction, that the product or service is functional and producible. It also provides a visual means to share the concept with others. The concept of a mechanical working model is easier to grasp and understand than software, e-commerce or service-related products. E-commerce models require verification of the ability to integrate the computers, servers, software and programming needed to support the operational concept. Services, packaged as a set of value-added activities, should deliver observable benefits.

Step 5.Market Study.

The Market Study is the next activity in the feasibility stage. The objective of the market study is to quantify the market assumptions you made in the market assessment of the initial concept investigation. In other words, who exactly is the target market, what are its characteristics, what competitive products does it currently use, how many do they use, what are the price points, how is the industry structured, how is the product distributed, what are the regulatory, environmental and economic factors, what are the barriers to market entry, and what will offer you a sustainable competitive advantage? The objective here is a thorough *quantitative* analysis.

Step 6.Business Feasibility.

Once the technical feasibility and market studies are completed, it is time to determine Business Feasibility. The first purpose of this effort is to financially model the venture opportunity and achieve a break-even analysis. In other words, based on the costs of goods sold, capital costs, and management and administration, how much revenue generated from units sold is required to break-even and over what period of time? Once a break-even analysis is developed, entrepreneurs can develop realistic financial projections for best and worst case scenarios. These scenarios will be critical in strategic planning, milestone development and venture valuation analysis. The simple objective is to determine what level of revenue is required to satisfy the return on investment demanded by the founder and/or the investors. This financial number or percentage will vary with economic conditions. During times of prosperity, the number will be higher because investors can get high-level returns in the stock market for much less risk. Early stage investors will look for a five to ten times return on their original investment. Later stage investors may view three to five times returns as acceptable.

If the revenues required to generate these types of returns are unrealistic or unjustifiable, the entrepreneur must stop and reconsider the venture opportunity. For instance, the most realistic revenue scenario might suggest it is unattractive to investors, yet is sufficient to meet the entrepreneur's personal objectives. In this case, entrepreneurs might consider growing the business more slowly than anticipated. This approach is called "bootstrapping" the company through reinvesting profits and deferring personal compensation until the venture is viable. The admonition is to choose the business and funding strategy that fits the numbers, but do not make the numbers fit a rigid business paradigm.

At this point, the entrepreneur should prioritize the business strategies that best fit the venture opportunity and pursue the most appropriate financing mechanisms. These will vary based on market considerations, such as life cycle of the product, speed to market, scope of launch (local, national or global) and attractiveness of the venture. Business strategies could include licensing, strategic alliances or partnerships, or a venture. Financing mechanisms could include debt or equity financing or a combination. Debt financing usually comes from institutional lenders while equity financing comes from other sources such as individual angel investors, venture capital, mergers, acquisitions or initial public offerings. High growth venture opportunities invariably utilize a variety and combination of financing mechanisms.

When the feasibility exercise is completed, the entrepreneur will have a plethora of technical, marketing and financial data, information, and supporting documentation. These resource materials will eventually be refined, distilled and integrated into the final business plan. For purposes of moving forward in the commercialization process, a concise executive summary of the information using a traditional business plan outline is sufficient to open discussions with potential seed stage/startup investors. However, there is still much work to do before the final business plan is ready for print.

Just because a deal may make money does not mean it is feasible. If, when the analysis is completed, the entrepreneur determines that a greater rate of return on investment can be made in stocks, bonds, or other low-to-moderate risk investments, *the exercise should be abandoned.* Some entrepreneurs are like the farmer who won the lottery. When asked what he intended to do with his winnings, the response was "I guess I'll keep on farming until all the money runs out!"

Development Phase

The entrepreneur has had one of those "eureka!" moments – an idea that is better than sliced bread – a better mousetrap. In addition, the entrepreneur has built a crude working model of the product, quantified the market opportunity, and determined the venture's economic feasibility. Now is the time to begin the Development Stage.

If the results of the Feasibility Stage are good and the feasibility is positive, the innovator now has sufficient information to attract outside investment to move forward in the commercialization process, predictably in the range of fifty thousand dollars to five hundred thousand dollars. This usually comes in the form of *seed capital* from an angel investor. These are typically wealthy individuals with an individual net worth in excess of one million dollars and annual incomes in excess of two hundred thousand dollars per year. These people are often called "smart money" investors. By and large, angel investors are savvy about the industry, the market and technology. More often than not, they have successfully launched, developed, and cashed out their own enterprises. Angel investors generally require an annualized rate of return in excess of thirty-five percent and a clearly defined exit strategy on how to cash out of the deal.

If, on the other hand, the entrepreneur has sufficient access to resources and capabilities in the value range of fifty thousand dollars to five hundred thousand dollars, an investor may not be required, but in either case, it will require significant resources to complete the next phase. The Development Phase consists of two stages: the Development Stage and the Introduction Stage.

Development Stage

The Development Stage involves the completion of three major activities: production of a limited amount of finished product or service, the strategic marketing plan, and the strategic business plan. This phase requires sufficient start-up capital to initiate business operations. For some ventures, this could be as little as a few thousand dollars, while others might need a million dollars or more. Needless to say, it is critical to have financing in place to accomplish this stage, which can take up to twelve months to complete.

Step 7.Engineering Prototype.

The objective of the Development Stage is three-fold: technical, market, and business *validation*. Technical validation is accomplished in the Engineering Prototype step. In the Development Stage, a limited amount of engineered product is introduced to the market. The finished product prototype, the primary technical objective of the Development Stage, is the single part, assembly, system, or service that accurately represents exactly what the final production units will eventually be in terms of 1) material content, 2) physical configuration, and 3) function. This limited amount or number of finished product or service provides the basis for final analysis of technical feasibility, cost, and market acceptance. From this product, final design and production specifications will be established. For a service-related product, the Development Phase involves a final test, or "beta" test, of the technical components of the system before launching operations. The single-part product or service is usually an expensive proposition due to the lack of economies of scale in production and the disproportionate design and testing costs attributable to the product.

Step 8.Strategic Marketing Plan.

The second step in the Development Stage is the Strategic Marketing Plan. During this step, the objective is to *validate* the market opportunity based on the assumption that the product or service can be delivered for a defined price and specifications to a willing buyer. This activity involves securing verifiable expressions of interest from potential distributors to market and sell the product and customers to buy it. The Strategic Marketing Plan provides a timeline associated with the key milestones, resources, and sales growth. The plan reflects the underlying marketing strategies the entrepreneur intends to implement in bringing the product to market, capturing market share, and growing sales. The Strategic Marketing Plan should closely reflect the assumptions and conclusions that were developed in the Economic Feasibility Stage.

Marketing activities in the Development Stage focus on making strategic decisions. The Strategic Marketing Plan includes final decisions on selecting the target market, determining product packaging, finalizing pricing, selecting optimal distribution channels, and determining sales and promotion methods and media. To accomplish this step requires working with a multitude of organizations such as packagers, wholesalers, retailers, shippers and advertisers, and consumer focus groups in some instances. When completed, the Strategic Marketing Plan in written form becomes a critical component of the final business plan.

Step 9.Strategic Business Plan.

The Strategic Business Plan reflects all the information, data and knowledge the entrepreneur has collected to date. It should accurately reflect the intent, rationale, conclusions, assumptions, risks and expectations concerning the business venture for the next five years. It could be shaped by input from or requirements by investors. At this point, it should be clear whether additional investment would be required to achieve the business opportunity.

If the business opportunity demonstrates a sales growth rate of thirty-five percent or greater per year, a dominant market position, and gross revenues of twenty-five million dollars or more by the fifth year, it could be a good candidate for follow-on financing by venture capital sources. Anything less with any one of these criteria could mean that an angel investor or bootstrap approach is in order. If an investor is needed and warranted, the business plan will need a section that includes information on the current value of the investment opportunity, the expected rate of investor return, anticipated uses of funds, and a payback strategy.

Once the Strategic Business Plan is completed and a determination is made that investment is required, it is advisable to obtain "sponsored" introductions to potential investors. The odds of securing an investor without a sponsored introduction are slim. The final business plan should be no more than twenty-five pages in length, including financials. Investors will base their decisions for present and future funding by this document.

At this point, critical decisions are made. Intellectual property issues are finalized, and many questions must be anticipated and answered, including the continuing role of the innovator in the new venture. Will it be as CEO or Chief Scientific Officer? Is it more advisable to license the opportunity or create an enterprise and launch the product? Is it better to pursue angel investors, venture capital, or bootstrap (self-finance) the venture? If outside capital is justified, what is the exit strategy for investors? Once these decisions are made, they are incorporated into a traditional written business plan and the capital campaign is launched if required.

If the business opportunity generates sufficient return on investment to satisfy the entrepreneur, but insufficient returns to stimulate outside investor interest, the entrepreneur is forced to consider bootstrapping the venture. This approach is often referred to as "the old, traditional way" of growing a business without outside investment. This could include maxing out credit cards, securing funds from friends and acquaintances, reinvesting earnings into the new business, deferring compensation, and/or establishing strategic partnerships and alliances. Once sufficient sales are achieved and assets are accumulated, the most common approach to funding the enterprise is debt financing through bank loans. More than fifty percent of start-ups use a debt financing approach, while equity alone finances one-third of start-ups.

If success requires a large amount of capital in a short period to achieve rapid and wide market penetration, venture capital often is the solution. Venture capitalists often get undeserved criticism from the founders of small companies who are horrified at venture capitalist terms and have no understanding of how venture capital markets work. The billions of dollars they invest each year are critical to the economy. In reality, less than five percent of investment opportunities demonstrate an appropriate level of sales, growth rates, and market opportunity to qualify for venture capital.

If the business offers sufficient returns to attract the attention of angel investors, but insufficient returns to meet venture capital criteria, angel investors will often "pony up" additional high risk, patient seed capital to position the business for high growth and profits. Angel investors often invest as a group.

Once the capital strategy is in place, the business is launched. Some start-ups typically have two hundred and fifty thousand or more invested before making their first sale. There is little margin for many missed steps. By this time, entrepreneurs have crawled far out on the limb; they have put faith in their assumptions that the limb will hold, but it is always good to have some assurance from those who are equally committed to the success of the business. Investors, whether venture firms, angels, or lenders can provide the enterprise with valuable assistance, insight, and experience to avoid these missed steps.

In the life of a venture-backed enterprise, there is a defining moment when the entrepreneur is momentarily on top of the world. It occurs when the lawyers for the investors and the entrepreneur complete the documentation and the first check is wired to the entrepreneur's bank account. It is truly a moment of exhilaration. It represents the culmination of months if not years of extremely hard work, sleepless nights, headaches, heartaches, and financial crisis. It is the end of an emotional roller coaster, at least until the next round of capital is required.

Reflecting back, the entrepreneur birthed a venture idea, proved its economic feasibility, developed the venture opportunity, and convinced investors to back the enterprise. Now the life of the business embarks on a new level of commercial activity – *venture introduction*, the fourth stage in the commercialization process.

Introduction Stage

The Introduction Stage consists of three activities: pre-production prototype, market validation, and business start-up. This stage can be considered the defining moment when the business is launched, limited amounts of product are produced, and limited sales are made. However, it is a rare venture that experiences a perfect launch – equipment setups are out of calibration, systems fail to integrate, suppliers are too early or late, advertising is wrong, or the bank fails to set up your line of credit. The objective is to work out the kinks as quickly as possible, maximize efficiencies, generate revenues, break-even financially and achieve profits.

Based on the desired features of the product as defined in the engineering prototype, a production and operational process, whether by people or machines, is put in place to achieve the objective of a reliable, manageable, and dependable system, or contracts are executed with outsourced providers. In either case, it is important to verify that the technical assumptions made in the business plan about the costs and capacities are valid.

Step 10. Pre-production Prototype.

The pre-production prototype step will result in knowledge about the manufacturability of the product, the manufacturing processes, maintainability and reliability, material and component lists, plans for field support, installation and production costs, safety and environmental factors, time schedules, and regulatory requirements. If it is a service product, the pre-production prototype will result in knowledge about the systems requirements, resource allocations, integration procedures, interoperability features, and customization needs. Once the assumptions are finally tested and validated, full production is launched and/or services are delivered.

Even though production is launched, no one would produce a million widgets without knowing whether the end-user was satisfied with the initial product. The market validation activity is designed to assess the market's receptivity to the product and to the overall effectiveness of the marketing process related to pricing, advertising, selling, distributing, and supporting the product. Constant monitoring of the market reaction from the target market, vendors, and competitors to the product introduction is critical. There are certainly critical adjustments to be made to capitalize and exploit early advantages or to correct early mistakes.

Step 11.Market Validation.

Market validation is not a haphazard process. It should be a well-defined project with specific outcomes. In addition to simply discovering the market's satisfaction level with the product, other marketing aspects should be discovered, such as the number of closings per contact, sales decision makers, the time for the sales cycle, the rate of sales growth, number of repeat sales, number of returns, customer satisfaction surveys, and many other market-related information needs.

Step 12.Business Start-up.

The business start-up activity can be simultaneously exhilarating and frustrating. It is a time to put in place the normal business systems essential to all enterprises such as human resources, accounting, communications, policies and procedures, legal, and planning. It is a time of adjustment related to team building, setting the foundation for a corporate culture, integrating and synthesizing skills and talent into a harmonious organization, and committing inordinate amounts of time and energy to the new enterprise.

In addition to the internal organizational development activities, the founding entrepreneur will discover tremendous amounts of time and energy planning for the future. While the emotional rollercoaster of securing the funding to create the company is now over, the Introduction Stage is analogous to launching the space shuttle. It takes a tremendous amount of fuel converted to energy to achieve lift off, and once the ship is off the launch pad, it must achieve tremendous acceleration and stay precisely on target to achieve the desired orbit. Any deceleration in propulsion or deviation from the course will result in disaster. Thus, the defining moment of venture development characterized by the first major round of investment capital is short lived, because good entrepreneurs always have their eye on the future and identify when the next round of capital will be needed, and what the company must accomplish to attract it.

The Commercial Phase

The last, longest, and defining phase of an entrepreneurial venture is the Commercial Phase. It represents the beginning of a journey toward great accomplishments and personal rewards, but above all, it is a journey designed to build and accumulate wealth. There are two stages to the Commercial Phase. One is the Early Growth Stage, followed by the Maturing Stage. It starts out first to grow the business, then to dominate a market niche and finally capture market share. The greater the size and dominance of the business translates into greater wealth. Once market position has been established, the enterprise can focus on maximizing financial value. This phase typically requires greater amounts of investment capital to move the product into new markets, increase production capabilities, add staff, and introduce new products. This is often satisfied by the venture capital market.

Growth Stage

The Growth Stage consists of the production, sales and distribution, and business growth activities. Whether the venture is designed as a lifestyle or high performance and growth company, the growth stage is designed to exploit the market opportunity and potential.

Step 13. Production.

The production activity involves the full-scale production. In today's competitive world, production activities must be cognizant of the soft production technologies involved with just-in-time manufacturing, supply chain optimization, e-procurement, lean manufacturing, and team-cell production. As commerce becomes more global, time-to-market, quality, and customer satisfaction have displaced price as the dominant economic imperative.

Step 14. Sales and Distribution.

The concept of sales and distribution grows more complex and more sophisticated each year, but the simple proposition in today's business world is – if you are not growing market share, you are probably in the cross hairs of your competitor's scope. This requires a systematic approach to monitoring product performance, customer profiles, and market positioning. The most sophisticated companies are utilizing extensive data collection and expert system software programs to provide them with the competitive intelligence to maximize their market opportunity.

Step 15. Business Growth.

Business growth ultimately depends on more than increasing sales. As the world segments into the old and new economy, it means businesses must be agile and early adopters of new business models and technologies. However, these activities must be accomplished without sacrificing the integrity of business systems and operations. To accomplish this feat requires the company to institutionalize strategic planning as a daily, dynamic process. This strategic planning activity must integrate with the overall enterprise management systems. The outcome of this activity should provide a set of critical performance indicators that monitor the health of the enterprise on a continuous, real-time basis. The Business Growth Stage often requires a management team with an entirely different set of skills than the entrepreneurial team that founded and launched the enterprise. As a result, it is not unusual to see a management turnover in a high performance company in the Growth Stage.

Maturity Stage

The final stage in the commercialization process is business maturity. The three activities of the Maturity Stage are production support, market diversification, and business maturity. Unlike most business models of the past, today's successful entrepreneurs have a specific exit strategy. Just as the skills, talents, and personalities of the founding entrepreneurs are often not a match for the growth stage management requirements, the same applies for the Maturity Stage. Growth management skills differ from those required of management charged with maximizing profits. In the past, many entrepreneurs conceived, formed and operated business operations without any plans for capitalizing on the venture's maximum value. Their exit strategy was to leave the business to their heirs, find a buyer, or liquidate the assets. Today's modern entrepreneurs plan on maximizing value by reinventing the company through new markets and new technologies on a continuous basis, positioning the company to be merged or acquired, growing the company through acquisitions, or completing an initial public offering. These strategies typically anticipate different management teams at various stages throughout the life of the venture to accomplish the objective of maximizing wealth.

Step 16. Product Support.

The life cycles of products today grow shorter each year. New designs, materials and manufacturing technologies result in continuous product improvement, modifications and displacements. Failure to perceive products and services as dynamic devices and perishable commodities that must maintain the customer's loyalty and satisfaction will result in a market opportunity for competition. Focusing on continually meeting customer needs and expectations in a continuously changing environment is a must. This means the product can change radically over time to the degree that it hardly resembles the original design and features.

Step 17. Market Diversification.

Someone once said, "Nothing happens until the sale is made." The sale triggers an avalanche of activities that potentially involve hundreds of people from all corners of the globe, with different languages and nationalities, different currencies, and even different forms of government. If sales are not growing and distribution channels are not extending and improving, the business could be nearing the end of a product's dynamic life cycle or losing market share to competing or disruptive products. In either case, it is time to consider whether it is reasonable to modify the product mix, find new markets, or look for new innovations. The market has the answers. The challenge is discovering the right questions to ask.

Step 18. Business Maturity.

When the business finally reaches an effective and efficient operational level and is achieving all the milestones envisioned, it is time to rethink the business plan. Recognize that the environment is continuously changing, and so should the business. The objective is to maximize the return on investment. Management should explore every opportunity to grow revenues and maximize the business value. At some point in time, one way or another, an exit strategy will occur. Hopefully, at the end of the day, the management and investors can each say in the words of the late Frank Sinatra, "I did it my way!"

Using the Commercialization Model – Step by Step

Launching a new business venture or a new product in an existing business is a risky proposition. Historically, innovators have reinvented the wheel of commercialization thousands and thousands of times. The utility of the commercialization model presented here has been tested and proven with more than two thousand start-up, Fortune 500, high-tech, biotech, energy, e-commerce and service companies. Companies using this model have raised more than five hundred million dollars in equity capital.

The Commercialization Model assists 1) entrepreneurs in identifying where they are in the commercialization process and priorities for next steps; 2) investors in assessing the venture readiness of an investment opportunity; 3) existing companies in developing new products for their portfolios; and 4) service providers in identifying when and where their services are most likely required. The initial step is identifying which phases, stages and steps have been accomplished in the commercialization process by the innovator.

Calculating a Venture Readiness Level

There are three questionnaires in the model: Technical Activities Questionnaire, Marketing Activities Questionnaire, and Business Activities Questionnaire. The questionnaires identify the technical, market, business and overall venture readiness levels of the commercial opportunity. Each questionnaire consists of six primary questions, with each primary question having supporting secondary questions. The responder answers yes/no to the list of questions in each questionnaire. The respective questionnaires will result in a Technical Readiness (TRL) score, Market Readiness (MRL) score and Business Readiness (BRL) score. If all of the supporting answers to each *key* question in the Technical Activities Questionnaire are positive, the TRL score for question 1 is "1.0". The maximum score for each question is 1.0 and the maximum total score to each questionnaire is 6.0.

For example, if the answer to question 1, *Have you completed an assessment of the technology?* is "yes," and the following seven questions (1.1 - 1.7) are "yes," the total score for the first question is "1.0 (100%)."

1. Have you completed an assessment of the technology? Yes.
1.1 Have you researched related patents or copyrights? Yes.
1.2 Have you researched technical journals and trade magazines? Yes.
1.3 Have you discussed the topic with experts? Yes.
1.4 Do you know the current state-of-the-art competitive technologies? Yes.
1.5 Have you selected the application for the technology? Yes.
1.6 Have you determined the advantages of this technology? Yes.
1.7 Have you determined the risks for this technology? Yes.

If *half* of the answers to the second question, *Do you have a working model of the product?* are positive, the TRL score for question 2 is "0.5 (50%)".

2. Do you have a working model of the product? Yes.
2.1 Have you evaluated the safety factors of the model? Yes.
2.2 Have you evaluated the environmental factors? Yes.
2.3 Have you evaluated the feasibility of producing the product? Yes.
2.4 Have you measured how the product will perform? No.

2.5 Do you have a design for the product? No.

2.6 Do you have a design for the production process? No.

If the following questions (3, 4, 5 and 6) are all answered "no," the total TRL score is calculated by adding all the scores together. In this case, the TRL score is $1.0 + 0.5 + 0 + 0 + 0 + 0 = 1.5$.

Once the TRL, MRL, and BRL scores are calculated, they are averaged for a total Venture Readiness Level Score. For example, if the final scores are: TRL = 1.5 (example above); MRL = 3.0; and BRL = 3.25, the final VRL score = $1.5 + 3.0 + 3.25 = 7.75 / 3 = 2.58$. This VRL score would suggest that the venture is: 1) a pre-product, pre-revenue stage company, and 2) a candidate for seed-stage financing and not venture capital financing.

Developing a Commercialization Strategy

The Commercialization Model follows a logical step by step process, based on the premise that each stage has a technical, market, and business step. Each step requires a series of activities to advance the business opportunity. Completing each step sequentially and thoroughly maximizes the probability that resources and efforts are expended efficiently and in a timely manner. However, it is commonplace for technical or engineering-oriented innovators initially to have positive answers for *significantly more* of the technical questions than the market and business questions. If the innovator has taken a balanced approach to commercialization, the number of questions with positive answers will be approximately the same in the technical, market, and business questionnaires.

Once the questionnaires are completed and the technical, market and business readiness levels are determined, the commercialization strategy can be developed. The first consideration should involve addressing answers and activities associated with the readiness level with the lowest level of accomplishment. This action enables the innovator to move the commercialization process back into the proper sequence. Once the missed or skipped steps are finished, the innovator can move forward in a logical sequence. It should be stressed that it is reasonable to work on multiple steps simultaneously, but be sure that each step represents a "go/no-go" decision step.

Again, it is most efficient to complete the steps in sequential order. Moving forward in the process without having positive indicators could be simply ignoring technical, market or business realities that are critical to success.

One benefit of the questionnaires can be realized during a review of the innovator's readiness levels. If the technical readiness level is significantly higher than the market and business readiness levels, it could mean the innovator's skills are stronger in the technical areas than in marketing and business. This outcome might indicate the innovator should solicit external marketing and business assistance in advancing the commercialization process.

It is very rare to find an innovator or entrepreneur who has all the skills required to launch a product or venture opportunity. It is always advisable to identify one or more service providers, mentors, investors, or other entrepreneurs who will offer candid observations and advice about assumptions, decisions, and progress.

The Venture Readiness Level (VRL) is important to entrepreneurs seeking investors in their business opportunity. Investment capital comes from a variety of sources for various reasons during the life of a venture. Friends and family are a source of investment, as are wealthy individual "angel" investors and venture capitalists. An entrepreneur is dependent upon his own resources and friends and family for opportunities with a VRL below 2.0. Angel investors usually invest in deals between 2.0 and 4.0, while venture capitalist make "early-stage" investments at VRL 4.0, "mid-stage" investments at VRL 5.0, and acquisitions and Initial Public Offerings at VRL 6.0.

With that introduction, you are ready to begin. Fill in the questionnaires. Analyze your readiness levels. Look at your response patterns. Sit down with an advisor and plan your commercialization strategy. Start with Step 1 in the Commercialization Model, and be sure to organize the information you collect because 1) it will eventually be voluminous, and 2) it will all be increasingly important as you progress through the commercialization process.

Technical Activities Questionnaire

(Circle the number of each question to which the answer is YES)

1.   Have you completed an assessment of the technology?

1.1   Have you researched related patents or copyrights?

1.2   Have you researched technical journals and trade magazines?

1.3   Have you discussed the topic with experts?

1.4   Do you know the current state-of-the-art competitive technologies?

1.5   Have you selected the application for the technology?

1.6   Have you determined the advantages of this technology?

1.7   Have you determined the risks for this technology?

2.   Do you have a working model of the product?

2.1   Have you evaluated the safety factors of the model?

2.2   Have you evaluated the environmental factors?

2.3   Have you evaluated the feasibility of producing the product?

2.4   Have you measured how the product will perform?

2.5   Do you have a design for the product?

2.6   Do you have a design for the production process?

3.   Do you have an engineering prototype of the product?

3.1   Have you identified what critical materials you will need?

3.2   Have you conducted final tests on the prototype?

3.3   Do you have a pilot production process?

3.4   Do you know how reliable the manufacturing will be?

4.   Do you have a production prototype of the product?

4.1   Have you conducted pilot production?

4.2   Have you selected the manufacturing process?

4.3 Have you selected the manufacturing equipment?

5. Do you conduct full-scale production?
5.1 Do you have a commercial-level design?
5.2 Have you produced sufficient quantities for market?
5.3 Have you established quality control procedures?
5.4 Have you finalized supply chain management procedures?

6. Do you support commercial production?
6.1 Do you have after market support for the product?
6.2 Have you improved the production process?
6.3 Do you support a warranty?

Marketing Assessment Questionnaire
(Circle the number of each question for which the answer is YES)

1. Have you assessed the needs of the market?
1.1 Do you know the product uniqueness?
1.2 Do you know the product competition?
1.3 Do you know the customer requirements?
1.4 Have you identified barriers to market entry?
1.5 Have you identified distribution channels?
1.6 Do you know the pricing criteria?

2. Have you conducted a market study?
2.1 Have you identified factors critical to the market environment?
2.2 Have you identified the economic and industry trends?
2.3 Have you quantified the market size?

2.4 Have you identified the market segments?

2.5 Have you identified the size, growth rate and competition of the market segment?

2.6 Have you analyzed business capability for market share, competitive position, product capabilities, and resource capabilities?

3. Have you defined the competitive advantages of the enterprise and the product?

3.1 Have you defined market objectives for the product, market image, service levels, market share, and sales levels?

3.2 Have you selected target markets?

3.3 Have you selected your market niche?

3.4 Have you selected product features?

3.5 Have you selected a price?

3.6 Have you selected distribution channels?

3.7 Have you obtained direct market feedback?

4. Have you conducted limited product sales?

4.1 Have you quantified the volume, rate, and demographics of sales?

4.2 Have you designed and implemented a customer survey?

4.3 Have you analyzed customer feedback (price, design, function, packaging, delivery)?

4.4 Have you analyzed your competitor's response?

4.5 Have you incorporated marketing modifications into the market plan?

4.6 Have you transmitted design modifications to technicians?

5. Have you established product distribution and sales?

5.1 Have you identified areas for market expansion?

5.2 Have you assessed customer satisfaction?

5.3   Have you assessed distributor satisfaction?

5.4   Have you refined product features?

5.5   Have you diversified your product line?

6.   Do you have a market environment scanning process?

6.1   Do you have a technology transfer and/or deployment process?

6.2   Do you make resource allocations for continual improvement?

6.3   Do you make resource allocations for new product development?

Business Activities Questionnaire

(Circle the number of each question to which the answer is YES)

1.   Have you self-assessed your entrepreneurial aptitude?

1.1   Does this venture appear to have profit potential?

1.2   Are you the right person to commercialize the product?

1.3   Is your enterprise the right one to commercialize the product?

1.4   Have you estimated the resources (capital and service providers) required to launch your venture?

1.5   Have you researched the intellectual property considerations?

2.   Have you developed a financial model and five-year revenue forecast for the business opportunity?

2.1   Does the venture demonstrate a positive economic feasibility?

2.2   Have you developed a break-even financial analysis for the venture?

2.3   Does the venture offer financial returns that justify investment?

2.4   Have you compared the merits of licensing to venturing?

3.   Have you secured initial funding to fund business start-up activities?

3.1 Have you developed a strategic business plan?

3.2 Have you finalized the intellectual property requirements?

3.3 Have you finalized the business organizational structure?

3.4 Have you selected a board of directors (or advisory team)?

3.5 Have you finalized agreements on any concurrent breakthrough?

3.6 Have you developed a formal financial plan that includes the strategy and timing of present and future funding rounds?

3.7 Have you developed a detailed business plan for product development including objectives, schedules, milestones and allocations of the required financial and human resources?

3.8 Can you ensure that management has critical experience and expertise in technology, product, market and business development?

3.9 Have you formed a cohesive commercialization team (design, manufacturing, marketing, management)?

4.   Have you initiated business activities?

4.1 Have you established hiring criteria?

4.2 Have you hired and trained core personnel?

4.3 Have you executed contracts?

4.4 Have you arranged for the next stage of financing?

4.5 Do you convene regular board of director meetings?

4.6 Have you developed a business policy and procedure manual?

4.7 Have you established control mechanisms for cash expenditures that correspond with the business plan?

4.8 Have you established a dynamic process for strategic and tactical planning for the enterprise?

5.   Are you engaged in full-scale production?

5.1   Have you arranged for full-scale production financing?

5.2   Have you institutionalized a corporate vision, mission, and policy?

5.3   Do you have a process to monitor business trends and practices?

5.4   Can you identify opportunities and threats to enterprise profits?

6.   Are you optimizing the company's profit potential?

6.1   Have you implemented an internal company diagnostic process?

6.2   Do you provide continuing education and training opportunities?

6.3   Do you explore alternate management technologies?

6.4   Do you reinvest profits?

6.5   Do you monitor product life cycles in the enterprise portfolio?

6.6   Do you monitor opportunities and threats to enterprise profits?

6.7   Can you identify opportunities and threats to enterprise profits?

6.8   Do you conduct strategic and tactical planning for the enterprise?

Commercialization Steps

Step 1. Technical Concept Analysis

The first activity to testing these new venture assumptions is to investigate the technical validity of the product. This step is called the technical concept analysis. To have commercial value, the product or service should solve a real world problem better, cheaper, or faster than existing solutions, and the feature advantages of the new product must be powerfully better than existing ones. You should remember that huge advertising budgets, aggressive marketing strategies, and fierce customer loyalty often support existing products and services. It is seldom enough for an incremental improvement in a product to displace a well-entrenched product already in the market. Also, remember that product benefits take precedence over product features. Customers buy electric drills to make holes, not to get fancy cases.

The purpose of this activity is to assess the intellectual property status of any technology involved in the product. This involves determining whether the product or any of its components are covered by intellectual property protection, such as patents or copyrights.

Definition: The process of determining that the physical features of the concept are potentially achievable and operational.

Objective: The objectives of the technical concept analysis step are to succinctly define the concept, to assess the implementation potential of the technical aspects of the concept, and to establish the uniqueness of the technical concept.

Product: The product of this activity is a verbal description, schematic, formula, conceptual model or paper design, delineating the main features of the technical concept.

Technical Activities: During the technical concept analysis step, the following activities must be completed:

- Define the concept fully;
- Demonstrate that performance assumptions are viable;
- Assess critical barriers to production;
- Survey the state-of-the-art of the technology; and
- Estimate the working models costs.

Technical Information: The technical concept analysis will usually result in knowledge about the features of the technical concept, performance expectations, prior art, and other similar or related research and development activities.

Assessment:
- Have you completed a technology database search?
- Have you researched related patents or copyrights?
- Have you researched technical journals and trade magazines?
- Have you discussed the topic with experts?
- Do you know the current state-of-the-art competitive technologies?
- Have you selected the technologies for the application?
- Have you determined the advantages of this technology?
- Have you determined the risks for this technology?
- Do the benefits of this technology or product offer significant advantages over the existing solution?

Step 2. Market Needs Assessment

Assuming all things are still positive, the next step is to investigate a marketing concept for the product. This step is called the market needs assessment. The questions are straightforward and simple: who will buy the product, how many will they buy, and how much will they pay? Discovering this information is not as simple as asking the questions. At this level of analysis, the information comes primarily from secondary sources such as trade journals, periodicals, existing market studies and electronic data. The permissible margin for error at this level is large. This activity is designed more to qualify the market opportunity than quantify it at this point in the process. The purpose here is to develop a level of confidence about the marketability of the product.

Definition: The process of determining whether the concept demonstrates superior ability over current solutions to meet a market need.

Objective: The objective of a market needs assessment is to identify a potential market for the concept, estimate the market size and determine a preliminary value of the product.

Product: The product of this step is a short summary of information from trade journals, databases, and interviews that follows the marketing section of a standard business plan format.

Marketing Activities: The marketing activities common to this step are those necessary to demonstrate that the product is unique and sustainable in a competitive marketplace.

During the conceptual phase, the following activities must be completed:
- Identify three unique features or benefits of the product;
- Identify the competition;
- Establish customer requirements for the product;
- Identify potential market barriers;
- Identify market distribution channels; and
- Identify product-pricing criteria.

Marketing Information: Completion of the conceptual marketing step will usually result in a rationale of why the product will receive a positive market response, gross estimates of the market and its segmentation, a simple explanation of how the product will be marketed, and an estimated price for the product.

Assessment:
- Have you assessed the needs of the market?
- Do you know the product uniqueness?
- Do you know the product competition?
- Do you know the customer requirements?
- Have you identified the barriers to market entry?
- Have you identified distribution channels?
- Do you know the pricing criteria?

Step 3. Venture Assessment.

When market research is completed and the entrepreneur is convinced the product can be made and that there is sufficient market demand to justify production, the final step of the investigation stage is the venture assessment. This step initially involves answering a series of questions in logical sequence: Does it make more sense to license this product opportunity to a company that can take it to market, or does the entrepreneur have the resources and ability to pursue a commercial venture? If the answer is "yes" to licensing, the next questions are: who are the potential licensees, how much additional development work is required to secure a license, and what are the standard license fees and royalty rates in the industry? If, on the other hand, the entrepreneur decides to pursue a venture, the next questions are: what experts are needed, how much and what kind of capital will be required, and what role will the founder play in the venture? The ultimate question is: will this venture opportunity generate sufficient return on investment to justify the risk?

Definition: The process of determining whether the business opportunity demonstrates profit potential.

Objective: The objective of the venture assessment is to determine if the concept offers sufficient profit potential to pursue additional investment of time and money for additional research.

Product: The product of this step is a brief description of the business model.

Business Activities: The research activities common to this step are those necessary to demonstrate that the concept will generate a profit and that the organization is capable of taking the product to market.

During the conceptual phase, the following activities must be completed:
- Identify financial, physical, and human resources required for commercialization;
- Identify the status of intellectual property requirements; and
- Establish a positive profit potential.

Business Information: Completion of the conceptual business step will usually result in an estimate of the revenues and costs of product sales, identification of source and use of capital for the development phase.

Assessment:
- Do you have experience in launching a business enterprise?
- Does this venture appear to have profit potential?
- Are you the right person to commercialize the product?
- Is your enterprise the right one to commercialize the product?
- Have you estimated the resources (capital and service providers) required to launch your venture?
- Have you researched the intellectual property considerations?

Step 4. Technical Feasibility

The first step in the Feasibility Stage, technical feasibility, involves the development of a working model of the product or service. It is not necessary for the initial materials and components of the working model to represent those that actually will be used in the finished product or service. The purpose of the working model is to demonstrate, to your own satisfaction, that the product or service is functional and producible. It also provides a visual means to share your concept with others. The concept of a mechanical working model is easier to grasp and understand than software, e-commerce, or service-related products. E-commerce models require verification of the ability to integrate the computers, servers, software, and programming needed to support the operational concept. Services, packaged as a set of value-added activities, should deliver observable benefits.

Definition: The process of proving that the concept is technically possible.

Objective: The objective of the technical feasibility step is to confirm that the product will perform and to verify that there are no production barriers.

Product: The product of this activity is a working model.

Technical Activities: During the technical feasibility step, the following must be completed:
- Test for technical feasibility;
- Examine the operational requirements;
- Identify potential safety and environmental hazards;

• Conduct a preliminary production feasibility assessment;
• Conduct a preliminary manufacturing assessment; and
• Estimate engineering prototype costs.

Technical Information: The technical feasibility will usually result in knowledge about the product or process design, performance, production requirements, and preliminary production costs.

Assessment:
• Do you have a working model of the product?
• Have you evaluated the safety factors of the model?
• Have you evaluated the environmental factors?
• Have you evaluated the feasibility of producing the product?
• Have you measured how the product will perform?
• Do you have a design for the product?
• Do you have a design for the production process?

Step 5. Market Study.

The market study is the next activity in the feasibility step. The objective of the market study is to quantify the market assumptions made in the market assessment of the initial concept investigation. In other words, who exactly is the target market, what are its characteristics, what competitive products does it currently use, how many do they use, what are the price points, how is the industry structured, how is the product distributed, what are the regulatory, environmental and economic factors, what are the barriers to market entry, and what will offer you a sustainable competitive advantage? The objective here is a thorough *quantitative* analysis.

Definition: The process of identifying the price range at which a quantified market segment is willing to purchase the product and justifying why the target market will chose the product over the competition.

Objective: The objective of the feasibility step is to identify who will buy the product, how many units will they buy, and how much they will pay.

Product: The product of this step is a market study that follows the marketing section of a standard business outline format.

Marketing Activities: The marketing activities common to this step are those necessary to demonstrate that there is market justification for the product.

During the market study step, the following activities must be completed:
- Describe the market environment;
- Identify economic and industry trends;
- Quantify the size of the market;
- Identify the market segments;
- Analyze market segment size, growth rate, competitive environment; and
- Analyze business capabilities for market share, competitive position, product capabilities, and resource capabilities.

Marketing Information: The completion of the marketing study step will usually result in a thorough understanding of the market environment, the market structure, the market potential for the product, a realistic expectation of market share, and the capabilities of the business enterprise to compete.

Assessment:

- Have you conducted a market study?
- Have you identified factors critical to the market environment?
- Have you identified the economic and industry trends?
- Have you quantified the market size?
- Have you identified the market segments?
- Have you identified the size, growth rate and competition of the market segment?
- Have you analyzed business capability for market share, competitive position, product capabilities, and resource capabilities?

Step 6. Economic Feasibility.

Once the technical feasibility and market studies are completed, it is time to determine the business feasibility. The first purpose of this effort is to financially model the venture opportunity and achieve a break-even analysis. In other words, based upon the costs of goods sold, capital costs, and management and administration, how much revenue generated from units sold is required to break-even and over what period of time? Once a break-even analysis is developed, the entrepreneurs can develop realistic financial projections for best case and worst-case scenarios. These scenarios will be critical in strategic planning, milestone development and venture valuation analysis. The simple objective is to determine what level of revenue is required to satisfy the return on investment demanded by the founder and/or the investors.

Definition: The economic feasibility step of business development is that period during which a break-even financial model of the business venture is developed, based on all costs associated with taking the product from idea to market and achieving sales sufficient to satisfy debt or investment requirements.

Objective: The objective of the economic feasibility is to develop a financial model of the business venture.

Product: The product of this step is a complete integration of the technical product information and the market study into one or more break-even financial models.

Business Activities: The business activities common to this step are those necessary to develop a conceptual plan for a business venture based upon one or more financial scenarios.

During the economic feasibility step, the following activities must be completed:

- Develop a financial analysis that identifies break-even scenarios based upon unit prices, volume of sales, and costs;
- Determine whether the business opportunity presents sufficient profit margins to justify a business venture; and
- Assess the merits of licensing the opportunity compared to venturing.

Business Information: Completion of the economic feasibility step will usually result in a go/no-go decision concerning the business venture, and if the decision is positive, identification of sources and uses of seed capital for the development phase.

Assessment:
- Does the venture demonstrate a positive economic feasibility?
- Have you developed a break-even financial analysis for the venture?
- Does the venture offer financial returns that justify investment?
- Have you compared the merits of licensing to venture?

Step 7. Engineering Prototype.

The objective of the Development Stage is three-fold: technical, market and business *validation*. Technical validation is accomplished in the engineering prototype step. In the Development Stage, a limited amount of engineered product is introduced to the market. The finished product prototype, the primary technical objective of the Development Stage, is the single part, assembly, system, or service that accurately represents exactly what the final production units will eventually be in terms of 1) material content, 2) physical configuration, and 3) function. This limited amount or number of finished product or services provides the basis for final analysis of technical feasibility, cost and market acceptance. From this product, final design and production specifications will be established. For a service-related product, the development phase involves a final test, or "beta" test, of the technical components of the system before launching operations. The single part product or service is usually an expensive proposition due to the lack of economies of scale in production and the disproportionate design and testing costs attributable to the product.

Definition: The process of identifying the most appropriate and efficient materials, processes, and designs suitable for commercial production to be incorporated into the product.

Objective: The objective of the engineering prototype is to make improvements in materials, designs, and processes in the product and to verify that the product will perform as specified.

Product: The product of this activity is an engineering prototype or a pilot process.

Technical Activities: During the engineering prototype step, the following activities must be completed:
- Identify materials, processes, components, and manufacturing steps required to meet technical performance and specifications;
- Test materials, components, processes;
- Design and construct a pilot process or engineering prototype;
- Optimize the design iterations;
- Conduct final tests; and
- Estimate pre-production prototype costs.

Technical Information: The engineering prototype will usually result in knowledge about the product specifications, the required manufacturing process to produce the product, proof of expected reliability, and refined production cost estimates.

Assessment:
- Do you have an engineering prototype of the product?
- Have you identified what critical materials you will need?
- Have you conducted final tests on the prototype?
- Do you have a pilot production process?
- Do you know how reliable the manufacturing will be?

Step 8. Strategic Marketing Plan.

The second step in the Development Stage is the strategic marketing plan. During this step, the objective is to *validate* the market opportunity based on the assumption that the product or service can be delivered for a defined price and specifications. This activity involves securing verifiable expressions of interest from potential distributors to market and sell the product and customers to buy it. The strategic marketing plan provides a timeline associated with the key milestones, resources, and sales growth. The plan reflects the underlying marketing strategies the entrepreneur intends to implement in bringing the product to market, capturing market share, and growing sales. The strategic marketing plan should closely reflect the assumptions and conclusions that were developed in the Economic Feasibility Stage.

Marketing activities in the Development Stage focus on making strategic decisions. The Strategic Marketing Plan includes final decisions on selecting the target market, determining product packaging, finalizing pricing, selecting optimal distribution channels, and determining sales and promotion methods and media. To accomplish this step requires working with a multitude of organizations such as packagers, wholesalers, retailers, shippers and advertisers, and consumer focus groups in some instances. The strategic marketing plan, in written form, becomes a critical component of the final business plan.

Definition: The process of making specific decisions concerning the marketing approach that will be incorporated into the business plan.

Objective: The objective of the strategic marketing step is to narrow the marketing decisions to those that offer the highest opportunity to maximize profitability.

Product: The product of this step is a concise marketing component of the business plan that reflects the optimum strategic business options for the enterprise.

Marketing Activities: The marketing activities common to this step are those necessary to the articulating a specific explanation on the marketing approach that the enterprise will use.

During the strategic marketing plan step, the following activities must be completed:
- Define competitive advantage of enterprise and product;
- Define marketing objectives (product, markets, image, service levels; business results like market share and sales levels);
- Select target markets;
- Identify target market niche;
- Select product features;
- Select price;
- Select distribution channels;
- Obtain direct market feedback; and
- Identify marketing team.

Marketing Information: The completion of the marketing study step will usually result in a comprehensive explanation of what and to whom the enterprise will market the product as well as when, where, and how the product will be marketed.

Assessment:

- Have you defined the competitive advantages of the enterprise and the product?
- Have you defined market objectives for the product, market image, service levels, market share, and sales levels?
- Have you selected target markets?
- Have you selected your market niche?
- Have you selected product features?
- Have you selected a price?
- Have you selected distribution channels?
- Have you obtained direct market feedback?

Step 9. Strategic Business Plan.

The strategic business plan reflects all the information, data, and knowledge the entrepreneur has collected to date. It should accurately reflect the intent, rationale, conclusions, assumptions, risks, and expectations concerning the business venture for the next five years. It could be shaped by input from or requirements of any investors. At this point, it should be clear whether additional investment will be required to achieve the business opportunity.

If the business opportunity demonstrates a sales growth rate of thirty-five percent or greater per year, a dominant market position, and gross revenues of twenty-five million dollars or more by the fifth year, it could be a good candidate for follow-on financing by venture capital sources. Anything less with any one of these criteria could mean that an angel investor or "bootstrap" approach is in order. If an investor is needed and warranted, the business plan will need a section that includes information on the current value of the investment opportunity, the expected rate of investor return, anticipated uses of funds, and a payback strategy.

Definition: The process of making sure that critical decisions concerning financing options, organizational structure, marketing approaches, and strategic partnerships are matched with the aspirations of the founders and the capabilities of the organization.

Objective: The objective of the strategic planning step is to identify and prioritize the business options, which optimize the opportunity for success.

Product: The product of this step is a concise business plan that reflects the optimum strategic business options for the enterprise.

Business Activities: The business activities common to this step are those necessary to develop a formal business plan.

During the Strategic Planning Stage, the following activities must be completed:
- Finalization of intellectual property requirements;
- Finalize business organization structure;
- Select a board of directors (or advisory team);
- Finalize agreements on any concurrent breakthrough technology requirements critical to commercialization;
- Develop a formal financial plan that includes the strategy and timing of present and future funding rounds;
- Develop a detailed business plan for the Product Development Stage including objectives, schedules, milestones and allocations of the required financial and human resources;

- Ensure that the management team has critical experience and expertise in technology/product/market and business development; and
- Form a cohesive commercialization team (design, manufacturing, marketing, management).

Business Information:Completion of the strategic planning step will usually result in a formal business plan, finalization of enterprise formation (or corporate commitment for implementation), finalization of intellectual property requirements, acquisition of pre-venture capital funding, and finalization product development agreements.

Assessment:
- Have you developed a strategic business plan?
- Have you finalized the intellectual property requirements?
- Have you finalized the business organizational structure?
- Have you selected a board of directors (or advisory team)?
- Have you finalized agreements on any concurrent breakthrough?
- Have you developed a formal financial plan that includes the strategy and timing of present and future funding rounds?
- Have you developed a detailed business plan for product development including objectives, schedules, milestones and allocations of the required financial and human resources?
- Can you ensure that management has critical experience and expertise in technology, product, market and business development?
- Have you formed a cohesive commercialization team (design, manufacturing, marketing, management)?

Step 10. Pre-Production Prototype.

The pre-production prototype step will result in knowledge about the manufacturability of the product, the manufacturing processes, maintainability and reliability, material and component lists, plans for field support, installation and production costs, safety and environmental factors, time schedules, and regulatory requirements. If it is a service product, the pre-production prototype will result in knowledge about the systems requirements, resource allocations, integration procedures, interoperability features, and customization needs. Once the assumptions are finally tested and validated, full production is launched and/or services are delivered.

Definition: The process of preparing the product for introduction into the marketplace.

Objective: The objective of the pre-production prototype is to develop the manufacturing processes and techniques required to produce the product.

Product: The product of this activity is a pre-production prototype or process.

Technical Activities: During the pre-production prototype step, the following activities must be completed:
- Develop a pre-production prototype;
- Determine pre-production processes;
- Select final product materials and components;
- Select manufacturing procedures, equipment, and tools;
- Assess specification conformance;

- Test product performance, reliability, and quality;
- Design a field support system; and
- Calculate full production costs.

Technical Information: The pre-production prototype step will usually result in knowledge about the manufacturability of the product, the manufacturing processes, maintainability and reliability, material and component lists, plans for field support, installation and production costs, safety and environmental factors, time schedules, and regulatory requirements.

Assessment:
- Do you have a production prototype of the product?
- Have you conducted pilot production?
- Have you selected the manufacturing process?
- Have you selected the manufacturing equipment?
- Have you conducted full-scale production?
- Do you have a commercial-level design?
- Do you have quality control procedures?
- Have you produced sufficient quantities for market?

Step 11. Market Validation.

Market validation is not a haphazard process. It should be a well-defined project with specific outcomes. In addition to simply discovering the market's satisfaction level with the product, other marketing aspects should be discovered, such as the number of closings per contact, names of sales decision makers, the time for the sales cycle, the rate of sales growth, number of repeat sales, number of returns, customer satisfaction surveys, and many other market-related information needs.

Definition: The process of introducing the product to the market, assessing market approaches, and obtaining customer feedback.

Objective: The objective of the market validation step is to test the receptivity of the market to the product and to compare expectations of the business plan with the realities of the marketplace.

Product: The product of this step is a quantitative analysis of limited sales performance and a qualitative analysis of customer response.

Marketing Activities: The marketing activities common to this step are those necessary to obtain a quantitative and qualitative market response to the product.

During the strategic marketing plan step, the following activities must be completed:
- Conduct limited product sales;
- Quantify the volume, rate, and demographics of sales;
- Design and implement a customer survey;

- Analyze customer feedback (price, design, function, packaging, delivery); and
- Transmit design modifications to technicians.

Marketing Information: Completion of the marketing validation step will usually result in a verification of the validity of the enterprise's marketing approach for the product and/or identification of recommended modifications.

Assessment:
- Have you conducted limited product sales?
- Have you quantified the volume, rate, and demographics of sales?
- Have you designed and implemented a customer survey?
- Have you analyzed customer feedback (price, design, function, packaging, delivery)?
- Have you analyzed your competitor's response?
- Have you incorporated marketing modifications into the market plan?
- Have you transmitted design modifications to technicians?

Step 12. Business Start-Up.

The business start-up activity can be simultaneously exhilarating and frustrating. It is a time to put in place the normal business systems essential to all enterprises, such as human resources, accounting, communications, policies and procedures, legal, and planning. It is a time of adjustment related to team building, setting the foundation for a corporate culture, integrating and synthesizing skills and talent into a harmonious organization, and committing inordinate amounts of time and energy to the new enterprise.

Definition: The business start-up step of business development is that period during which business functions (management, production, financing, legal, marketing, and human relations) are initiated by key personnel.

Objective: The objective of the business start-up step is to introduce the enterprise to the market within the parameters identified in the business plan.

Product: The product of this step is an enterprise capable of producing a product that meets technical and customer specifications, satisfies customer expectations, and demonstrates a potential profit.

Business Activities: The business activities common to this step are those necessary to introduce the product to the market, establish a foundation for sound business practices, and implement a growth strategy.

During the business start-up step, the following activities must be completed.

- Establish hiring criteria;
- Hire and train core personnel;
- Execute limited contracts;
- Arrange for next stage financing;
- Regularly convene board of director meetings;
- Develop business policy and procedure manuals;
- Establish control mechanisms for cash expenditures that correspond with the business plan; and
- Establish a dynamic process for strategic and tactical planning for the enterprise.

Business Information: Completion of the business start-up step will usually result in knowledge gained from the establishment of business functions, introduction to the market, assessment of market response, and confirmation of profitability, identification of required technical, marketing and business modifications and refinements.

Assessment:

- Have you initiated business activities?
- Have you established hiring criteria?
- Have you hired and trained core personnel?
- Have you executed contracts?
- Have you arranged for the next stage of financing?
- Do you convene regular board of directors meetings?
- Have you developed a business policy and procedure manual?
- Have you established control mechanisms for cash expenditures that correspond with the business plan?
- Have you established a dynamic process for strategic and tactical planning for the enterprise?

Step 13. Production.

The production activity involves full-scale production. In today's competitive world, production activities must be cognizant of the soft production technologies involved with just-in-time manufacturing, supply chain optimization, e-procurement, lean manufacturing, and team-cell production. As commerce becomes more global, time-to-market, quality, and customer satisfaction have displaced price as the dominant economic imperative.

Definition: The production step is that period during which the manufacturing process is built and full-scale production runs are implemented.

Objective: The objective of the production step is to put a new product into commercial production and optimize the manufacturing process.

Product: The product of this activity is a market-ready product.

Technical Activities: During the production step, the following activities must be completed:
- Final commercial level product designs;
- Produce manufacturing process schematics;
- Institute quality control procedures;
- Finalize distribution system;
- Construct manufacturing facilities;
- Implement trial run;
- Make minor modifications; and
- Conduct full-scale production run.

Technical Information: Completion of the production step will usually result in knowledge about production levels and costs, inventory requirements, manpower allocations, production bottlenecks, vendor requirements, distribution factors, manufacturing reliability and maintainability, and product performance and reliability.

Assessment:
- Do you support commercial production?
- Do you have after-market support for the product?
- Have you improved the production process?
- Do you support a warranty?

Step 14. Sales and Distribution.

The concept of sales and distribution grows more complex and more sophisticated each year, but the simple proposition in today's business world is – if you are not growing market share, you are probably in the cross hairs of your competitor's scope. This requires a systematic approach to monitoring product performance, customer profiles, and market positioning. The most sophisticated companies are utilizing extensive data collection and expert system software programs to provide them with the competitive intelligence to maximize their market opportunity.

Definition: The sales and distribution step is that period when the product is receiving some degree of market reception by distributors and buyers.

Objective: The objective of the sales and distribution step is to gain market share and increase profitability.

Product: The product of this step is a final confirmation or modification of one or more elements in the marketing approach.

Marketing Activities:The marketing activities common to this step are those necessary to expand product sales and assess the product's market performance.

During the sales and distribution step, the following activities must be completed:
- Identify areas for market expansion;
- Assess customer satisfaction;
- Assess distributor satisfaction; and
- Refine product features.

Marketing Information: Implementation of the sales and distribution step will usually result in a knowledge of the product's competitive position in the market, the demographics of the product, key customers for the product, perceived benefits of the product, proper communication mechanism for promoting the product, and the most effective and efficient sales channels.

Assessment:
- Have you established product distribution and sales?
- Have you identified areas for market expansion?
- Have you assessed customer satisfaction?
- Have you assessed distributor satisfaction?
- Have you refined product features?

Step 15. Business Growth.

Business growth ultimately depends on more than increasing sales. As the world segments into the old and new economy, it means businesses must be agile and early adopters of new business models and technologies. However, these activities must be accomplished without sacrificing the integrity of business systems and operations. To accomplish this feat requires that the company institutionalize strategic planning as a daily, dynamic process. This strategic planning activity must integrate with the overall enterprise management systems. The outcome of this activity should provide a set of critical performance indicators that monitor the health of the enterprise on a continuous, real-time basis. The Business Growth Stage often requires a management team with an entirely different set of skills than the entrepreneurial team that founded and launched the enterprise. As a result, it is not unusual to see a management turnover in a high performance company during the Growth Stage.

Definition: The business growth phase is that period during which business functions (management, production, financing, marketing, and human relations) are fully staffed and operational.

Objective: The objective of the business growth phase is to operate a business enterprise which produces a profitable product for which there is increasing market demand.

Product: The product of this phase is a business enterprise that the market perceives is a preferred source for the product and/or service.

Business Activities: The business activities common to this phase are those necessary to establish a foundation of sound business practices, implement a growth strategy, and ensure profitability.

During the business growth step, the following activities must be completed:
- Obtain equipment and facilities;
- Hire and train personnel;
- Execute contracts;
- Arrange for next stage financing;
- Institutionalize management vision, mission, and policies;
- Regularly convene board of directors meetings;
- Monitor industrial business trends and practices;
- Identify opportunities and threats to enterprise profits; and
- Conduct strategic and tactical planning for the enterprise.

Business Information: The business growth phase will usually result in knowledge of market receptivity to the enterprise, price-value threshold of product, competitor response, emerging competition, critical factors for enterprise operating success.

Assessment:
- Are you engaged in full-scale production?
- Have you arranged for full-scale production financing?
- Have you institutionalized a corporate vision, mission, and policy?
- Do you have a process to monitor business trends and practices?
- Can you identify opportunities and threats to enterprise profits?

Step 16. Production Support.

The life cycles of products today grows shorter each year. New designs, materials, and manufacturing technologies result in continuous product improvement, modifications, and displacements. Failure to perceive products and services as dynamic devices and perishable commodities that must maintain the customer's loyalty and satisfaction will result in a market opportunity for your competition. Focusing on continually meeting customer needs and expectations in a continuously changing environment is a must. This means the product can change radically over time to the degree that it hardly resembles the original design and features.

Definition: The product support step is that period during which the product or process realizes a useful life.

Objective: The objective of the production support step is to maintain maximum value of the product or process through continual improvement in the technical aspects of the production process.

Product: The product of this activity is a competitive product.

Technical Activities: During the product support step, the following activities must be practiced:
- Produce on-site technical instructions and updates for safe and effective use of the product or process;
- Prepare, distribute and encourage use of instruction manuals for the assembly, operation, and maintenance of the product or process;
- Design, produce, and distribute "consumables" used in the product or process;

- Design and introduce timely, but minor improvements in materials, components, systems, and software;
- Produce and distribute spare parts;
- Set up and provide warranty services;
- Introduce new applications developed for the product or process;
- Identify new product spin-offs or major product design changes that would require going back into earlier stage to be re-identified as a new product; and
- Disseminate alerts and undertake remedial action for unplanned product deficiencies or changing safety and environmental requirements.

Technical Information: The production support step will usually result in knowledge about the optimal conditions, technologies, processes, and procedures to produce a competitive product.

Assessment:
- Do you support commercial production?
- Do you have after-market support for the product?
- Have you improved the production process?
- Do you support a warranty?

Step 17. Market Diversification.

The sale triggers an avalanche of activities that potentially involve hundreds of people from all corners of the globe, with different languages and nationalities, different currencies, and even different forms of government. If sales are not growing and distribution channels are not extending and improving, the business could be nearing the end of a product's dynamic life cycle or losing market share to competing or disruptive products. In either case, it is time to consider whether it is reasonable to modify the product mix, find new markets, or look for new innovations. The market has the answers. The challenge is discovering the right questions to ask.

Definition: The market diversification step is that period when the product is modified to meet new market opportunities or when new products are developed to meet existing market demand.

Objective: The objective of the market diversification step is to address changing market conditions.

Product: The product of this step is a portfolio of competitive products and multiple markets for products that insulate the enterprise against economic downturns.

Marketing Activities: The marketing activities common to this step are those necessary to diversify the products and markets.

During the market diversification step, the following activities must be accomplished:

- Market environment scanning process;
- Technology transfer and/or deployment processes;
- Allocation of resources for continued improvement of existing products; and
- Allocation of resources for new product development.

Marketing Information: Implementation of the market diversification step will more over result in knowledge of emerging industries, emerging products, emerging technologies, sources of technology, identification of new enterprise opportunities and threats, and resources for technical assistance in technology development and deployment.

Assessment:

- Have you diversified your product line?
- Do you have a market environment scanning process?
- Do you have a technology transfer and/or deployment process?
- Do you make resource allocations for continual improvement?
- Do you make resource allocations for new product development?

Step 18. Business Maturity.

When the business finally reaches an effective and efficient operational level and is achieving all the milestones envisioned, it is time to rethink the business plan. The environment is continuously changing; so should the business. The objective is to maximize the return on investment. Management should explore every opportunity to grow revenues and maximize the business value. At some point, one way or another, an exit strategy will occur.

Definition: The business maturity step is that period during which the enterprise secures market position, optimizes investment opportunities, and explores product and market diversification.

Objective: The objective of the business maturity step is to optimize the profit potential of the enterprise.

Product: The product of this activity is a business enterprise that is generating increasing profits through multiple revenue streams.

Business Activities: Activities common to business maturity are related to investment options and business decisions that ensure enhanced competitiveness.

During the business maturity phase, the following activities must be completed:
- Implement a company diagnostic process;
- Provide continuing education and training programs;
- Explore alternate management technologies;

- Invest profits;
- Monitor life cycles of product in enterprise portfolio;
- Regularly convene board of director meetings;
- Monitor industrial business trends and practices;
- Identify opportunities and threats to enterprise profits; and
- Conduct strategic and tactical planning for the enterprise.

Business Information: The business maturity step will usually result in knowledge of potential exit strategies, opportunities for business diversification, emerging industry changes, new market demands and expectations.

Assessment:
- Are you optimizing the company's profit potential?
- Have you implemented an internal company diagnostic process?
- Do you provide continuing education and training opportunities?
- Do you explore alternate management technologies?
- Do you reinvest profits?
- Do you monitor product life cycles in the enterprise portfolio?
- Do you monitor opportunities and treats to enterprise profits?
- Can you identify opportunities and threats to enterprise profits?
- Do you conduct strategic and tactical planning for the enterprise?

Conclusion

The commercialization process is never straightforward nor is it easily accomplished. Throughout history, successful companies have invented ways and continually reinvented themselves to be relevant to their customers. It is my hope for you, whether you are a startup or an existing company, for this material to continue to benefit you in your commercial journey.

LaVergne, TN USA
01 September 2010
195567LV00001B/12/P

9 780615 312736